Don't Be Invisible Be Fabulous
Volume 5

Realizing You Are Enough

Compiled by

Dorris Burch

Don't Be Invisible Be Fabulous, Volume 5: Realizing You Are Enough

Published by Fab Factor Publishing
Tinley Park, IL

ISBN: 978-0-578-75389-8

Cover design, layout, and typesetting:
Fab Factor Publishing

Cover photo: Charles Taitt

For you....

If you're called to join women around the world and say YES to adding more purpose, meaning and fabulousness into your life, then

My intention is to gift you the opening you require to say YES to you at a higher level. To embody your heartfelt desires AND your Soul's calling. To let go of the guilt, the burden and the unnecessary fear that can so easily stop us from our next level of truth.

CONTENTS

THE FABULOUS
DORRIS BURCH

INTRODUCTION

I "consider" myself spiritual and awake. I teach women how to surrender, how to trust their desires so they may receive what they require. I talk constantly about the 'highest version you...'

I remember longing to be the woman I came here to be...to know I was HER!

You know when you want something so bad it hurts? When you have a message inside of you, and you want to make sure it is expressed clearly and that it has the impact it is meant to have? I wanted to live all of me. I wanted to live my FULL POTENTIAL.

"It's no longer working", I allowed myself to finally say it out loud, with almost a deep cry. I instantly felt relief followed by a compounding fear. *"What did this mean? How was this going to affect everything?"*

I knew it was time to leave my corporate career and answer the calling inside of me to become the highest version me. There is a knowing inside that you are capable, worthy, powerful and deserving and yet sometimes, we are 'clouded' in the fear that what if we are wrong, what if we really aren't all that? But what if you are? What if you could allow yourself to experience the fullness of your truth? What if you could grant yourself permission to follow your intuition, step into the most authentic part of who you are and let the approval of others no longer be what stops you from being...YOU?

I felt a deep calling to have the time to tap into more of who I really was. I longed for time to explore my deepest desires, to reconnect with who I was meant to be in this world...beyond being a daughter, a mom, a wife, a corporate girl...

I wanted to know...

- I be of service and use my unique gifts and talents?
- WHERE was the magic, the grace and the joy for me?

And one day...ONE thing changed: I became UNAVAILABLE to be unclear on exactly what my purpose was. I made the decision that I was going to be the woman who did whatever it took to get clear and confident on my calling. I connected with Spirit, deepened my femininity, transformed my money story, understood my family programming, and then had the confidence to create the business to put out in the world and FINALLY be of service! AND it worked!!!

I created a unique process of discovery that allowed me to AWAKEN to the woman I was truly called to be, and the MAGIC returned! Inside of this spirit-led process, I opened to new truths, new desires, a new awareness of who I was called to be by Spirit...my life became clear and guided. On the other end, I came out a woman with a purpose. With confidence. With deep self-love. With something to share with other women who wanted to make a dramatic shift as well. I was called to create a powerful process for other women seeking the MAGIC in their own lives. So they too could come out the other side knowing who they are and why they were here, knowing their unique gifts and talents.

There were moments I wanted to give up, times I thought about running away… And many, many times I questioned my own sanity. So many times, we (and by we...includes me too) hide from what we really want. What we REALLY desire. We don't say it out loud because we are scared...scared we will be laughed at, scared we won't get it. When our Fab Factor is not in sync, we come up with as many excuses as it takes to keep us from saying yes to our desires.

Sometimes, we don't allow ourselves to even feel our desires...much less ask for them. We don't even ask for what we really want. A lot of women struggle because they are living their life based on other people's expectations. Even women who are incredibly 'successful' find themselves feeling trapped and unable to trust their true desires. We all have had struggles and moments in our life where we doubt that "it" (whatever "it" is for you)...is possible.

Take it from someone who waited WAY TOO LONG, there will never be a better time to answer the questions that are keeping your life at a stand-still… Your best years are still ahead of you, it's just up to you to make the decision that you are willing to be of service in a BIG WAY. Give yourself permission to create the most fabulous possible life for not just yourself, but everyone else around you.

If you are feeling any piece of this in your life right

now, you are going to love the stories these eight fabulous women share with you… about their journey and what it really has taken for them to step into a life that reflects the truth of who they are…

Realizing You Are Enough

Remember –

Don't Be Invisible. Be Fabulous!

The Fabulous Dorris Burch

FOLLOW

THE LEAD

You are never too old.

"When the business got challenging such as in 2017 I learned how to adapt and change"
- Denise Lahav

DENISE LAHAV

I am going to start by telling a story within a story that may seem unrelated. On Wednesday evening I was out walking my dog and as we were walking on the sidewalk I came upon a baby chick sitting on the sidewalk chirping and I could tell it was injured. I couldn't get too close because my dog has a tendency to put little critters in her mouth. I have had to pry open her pitbull jaws and take out birds and rats. I almost felt this bird was pleading with me and looking at me personally. I went home and put my dog in her crate and went back with a shoebox and picked up the chick. I've never rescued a bird and everything fell into place and I was able to deliver the bird the next day to someone who could help him/her. I found the right people at the right time who told me where to keep and how to feed the chick overnight. It also worked out perfectly in the scheduling because there was someone coming in from out of town the next evening to pick up mockingbirds that needed rescue. So everything just fell into place and I felt led to the right people at the right time. I thought it was a pigeon but at some point, I texted the bird's photo to someone who told me it was a mockingbird chick, which helped as the care for a mockingbird is different than for a pigeon.

This is how I was led in business where being in the right place at the right time and listening to the prompts and nudgings led me in a certain direction that I never would have imagined myself going in before it actually happened. My encounter with this chick, although it was just overnight, has changed my life as the people and events that led to starting the business I am in now did. Because of the nature of my business, if I had thought I was too old to do this, I would not have moved forward. I am currently 66 years old and I'm in an industry that is usually reserved for people in their 20s and perhaps 30s.

To go back to my history that led me in my current direction, when I was a very young child I was obsessed with ballet. My goal in life was to become a ballet dancer and I took classes and constantly practiced at home. I was thought of by others as the best in my class. I was living in West Los Angeles and had a classic Russian dance instructor who helped shape me into becoming a great student and accomplished dancer at my level. When I was 11 years old we moved to another area of Los Angeles and I could not find the same type of school, instructor, and mentorship that I had previously. Out of discouragement, I quit ballet. It was something I was always sorry about and I regretted that I didn't stick with it and follow my passion to have a career in dance.

Although I didn't pursue a career in classical dance, dance was still my number one passion and from the time I was a child up until an adult, I constantly took a variety of dance classes. Although I was a professional belly dancer in my 20's, I still felt the lingering disappointment of having quit ballet.

Fast forward to 2009 where my dance activities mainly involved social dancing such as Ballroom and Latin. I was at the community college taking other classes and while there also enrolled in a Ballroom dance class. I met another dance instructor who invited me to do what she described as surprise crowd dancing. I accepted and thus the whole summer of 2009 I danced in a series of what I later found out were flash mobs on Fremont Street Experience, which is a tourist destination in Las Vegas. I had the summer of my life and fell in love with the whole process. Had I not met this dance instructor or said yes to her invitation, my life would not be what it is right now.

Once the summer was over this instructor did not continue producing flash mobs. I then serendipitously found out through a local friend on Facebook about a group in Los Angeles, Flash Mob America. I would time my visits to see my mother who lives in Los Angeles around their events. We did a couple of flash mobs that were on TV such as on the Bachelorette show. After a while, I wanted to do something locally. I had a background in event planning and knew quite a few people in different genres of the dance community thus decided to start my own group, Flash Mob Las Vegas.

One of my personality quirks is at the birth of a new idea about what I want to do I dig in my heels and procrastinate. I take halting steps and the momentum is slow. I hesitate being swept up in a tide I can't contain. Once I decided to form Flash Mob Las Vegas I dipped in one toe, pulled it out, and recoiled after I started a Flash Mob Las Vegas Facebook page and after months of stalling people started posting comments about when our events would be, like saying, "come on already!"

At some point, later on, I set up a website and what must be six months later decided to do our first event for a yearly Las Vegas downtown parade called Helldorado Days. Rather than do a flash mob, we did a dance march formation with a banner in front of the group to announce ourselves to the community. I didn't know what and if it would lead to anything, but it was my way of finally stepping out – literally!

I teamed up with a country dance teacher I knew, as Helldorado is country themed, and we choreographed a dance march to a Country Western song. As I was involved with the College of Southern Nevada (CSN) dance program I recruited students who were part of the dance club to add a step dance routine to our performance. We all dressed country, dance marched in the parade with our banner with our name and logo in front of the formation. It was a great first experience.

IT IS NEVER TOO LATE

On March 11, 2011, a 9.0/9.1 earthquake struck off the Pacific coast in Tohoku Japan which caused a devastating tsunami killing thousands. The tsunami caused a nuclear accident in Fukushima. This was the largest earthquake ever recorded in Japan and fourth-largest since modern recordkeeping began. I was moved to do something to help and discovered that a group I was associated with from my experience doing flash mobs in Los Angeles was doing a Japan relief flash mob. I asked if we could collaborate to do the same flash mob simultaneously with theirs in Las Vegas. So our first official dance flash mob was born. I wasn't sure who was going to teach it and approached my modern dance instructor at CSN and she agreed. The Los Angeles group shared their choreography and music, which was especially composed for this event, and CSN and local studios donated space for the rehearsals. A friend who is a CSN photography student agreed to videotape the event and his wife took photos. An idea popped into my head to invite a local Taiko drum group to join us and they agreed. We also found a great location, Tivoli Village shopping center that agreed to host our Flash Mob. We collected donations from the participants that went to an organization that helped provide formula and diapers to affected babies in the region of the earthquake and tsunami. At the same time as our flash mobs in Los Angeles and Las Vegas, or a participant joined us with the same choreography in Japan. It was touching that a collaborative video was produced which included all three of the flash mobs.

Through the experience of these first two events, I was reminded that once I decide to move forward, all the parts and players fall into place. Whether it was the instructors, choreography, music, rehearsal spaces, participants, and location, everything lined up. Although I hesitate in the beginning, once I get going there is no stopping me.

Our first event at the Helldorado Parade did end up leading to another community event. After seeing us at the parade, the Las Vegas Metropolitan Police Department Northeast Command contacted us to do a flash mob for National Night Out on August 2, 2011, at the Walnut Recreation Center right next to the command station. The department requested that we do a flash mob to promote fitness and it was perfect timing during First Lady Michelle Obama's Let's Move initiative to battle childhood obesity. We chose the song by Beyonce, "Move Your Body" that Michelle Obama danced to on an ABC News YouTube video on May 5, 2011.

I went to a meeting at the Northeast Command and they agreed to help us with a rehearsal space. I found College of Southern Nevada students to help teach and a squad of cheerleaders joined us. We had a large diverse group and had the best time being part of this event. The police were super to work with.

After doing these three events I realized how time consuming it was to produce a flash mob. I originally was not thinking of doing it as a business but realized the organizing took too much time away from my income producing activities. So I decided that if I was going to continue to organize flash mobs, people would have to hire me to produce them. No sooner did I think this than I got my first inquiry for a corporate flash mob. I received a request for a company that was doing a trade show at the Mandalay Bay Convention Center who wanted to do an Elvis style wedding flash mob to celebrate their merger with another company.

Not only was this my first time doing a corporate event but I also had the challenge of hiring an Elvis singer for the first time, plus dealing with costuming and hiring paid performers. I hired the College of Southern Nevada instructor who did our Summer of '69 flash mobs on Fremont Street Experience and two of the professional dancers who I know from those flash mobs and the college to be the lead performers. It was a great first experience doing a corporate event and a success.

That fall we continued to get requests for corporate events such as conferences and meetings. Since that time we have done flash mobs for major companies such as DuPont, Qualys, and Cisco Systems.

In 2012 we were approached by the Las Vegas Motor

Speedway to do a flash mob for the opening race day Sunday for NASCAR Weekend. I brought in a group of breakdancers to start the flash mob followed by three professional couples doing lifts and adagio.

We also did flash mobs for community events. I often got requests to donate flash mobs for charity events and decided I would do two events a year to support causes. We did flash mobs for AIDS Walk, Prevent Child Abuse Nevada and more.

At the end of 2011, there were two flash mobs done for marriage proposals by other companies, which went viral on YouTube. At that time I received our first request to do a marriage proposal. It was a great set up where the young lady being proposed to danced in the flash mob thinking that the flash mob was for someone else. Her boyfriend pulled her out of the group to propose after the dance.

Our second marriage proposal flash mob was in early 2012 for a couple from Singapore on Fremont Street Experience and included their photo and text on the Viva Vision screen which is a huge digital screen spanning that area of Fremont Street. We continued to do marriage proposal flash mobs and presently they are the mainstay of our business. We have done proposals for couples from all over the US, Europe, Asia, and Mexico. We have also done a few for gay couples as more regions legally supported marriage equality. I never got tired of doing them and after hundreds, I still cry.

In 2014, I got an email inquiry asking if we did splash mobs. I had no idea what a splash mob was but said yes and then googled it and found splash mob videos on YouTube. They are flash mobs where the performers jump in a pool and dance fully clothed, usually at a reception or other events done poolside. We did our first splash mob for Qualys at the Four Seasons. It was a new experience choreographing to dance in a pool as most movement is done with the upper body. Even finding a pool to rehearse in was a challenge, which we were able to figure out. From that point on we did splash mobs at major resorts for high profile clients. Out of this, I learned to just say yes and then figure it out.

2014 was our biggest year as far as the amount of flash mobs. When I started the business in 2011, I did not expect for it to last that long as I knew that flash mobs were a trendy phenomenon. Starting in 2015 the amount of flash mobs per year started to slowly decline but in 2017 they came to an abrupt halt. 2017 started with losing my beloved dog on January 1 and to also have a business fold added to the heartbreak. Done with all the fun and engagement of coordinating the events.

It wasn't that I didn't get inquiries; it was that when I got them, they didn't book. I was used to booking a high percentage of the requests. In addition to my flash mob business falling flat, the network marketing company I was also working with closed the doors to direct sales and went retail thus eliminating their independent consultants. All my business income stopped and all I could do was move forward to a solution.

FOLLOW YOUR PASSIONS

I looked inward and saw that my heart was not in organizing the flash mobs anymore. Perhaps I just needed the time and space to grieve undistracted. Starting in 2018

I started to delegate the organizing to my main choreographer Julie. When I got inquiries in 2017, I was not able to book them, which was unusual. Prior I booked a high percentage of inquiries. I thought perhaps people were sensing my turn off. I started to turn the leads over to Julie to respond, quote, book and then do the arrangements such as casting, booking the studio, and searching for a performance location.

Beginning in 2011 we did a Thriller Flash Mob every Halloween season. After our 2017 Thriller Flash Mob, I realized I really didn't want to continue to organize them so that was our last one. It turns out that other instructors and organizers in town we're doing Thriller so I had been able to send or zombie dancers elsewhere in 2018 & 2019. With these changes, I honored my boundaries thus freeing up space for things to keep flowing. I saw that by eliminating my own negative energy and reluctance things opened up.

Things started to shift in 2018 and the flash mobs started to happen again and by the end of the year, we started averaging two flash mobs a month. Although this was not the volume we were used to, it was great to start having them on a regular basis again. We do not do as many corporate events is in the past and now most of our flash mobs are private special occasions such as marriage proposals, birthdays, and some weddings.

This year Julie and I decided to capitalize on the marriage proposal business and started a new company, Pop the Question Las Vegas where we will offer other types of custom marriage proposal planning in addition to flash mobs. We are also going to expand into providing entertainment for other types of romantic events such as weddings and anniversaries.

I am happy that I was able to figure out a solution to resurrect a flash mob business. Although I don't take as much money from the bookings, as I am not doing as much of the work, it is great just to relax and show up and dance. I am happy to give Julie and professional performers opportunities to earn money plus provide more fun for our volunteer performers.

I am thankful for the experience the Flash Mob Las Vegas business has given me. I have made wonderful friends and business partners and have learned so much. I had to figure out how to do many things such as edit music, videos, and promoting events on Facebook. In the beginning, I started on new territory as far as booking studios, working with the venues and vendors. As it has been great to earn an income with what I am passionate about. When the business got challenging such as in 2017, I learned how to adapt and change. I look forward to seeing what fun will unfold in the future.

Addendum: It is now May 2020 and we are in the middle of the COVID 19 pandemic quarantine. As a flash mob is all about social closeness in public places, all of our potential bookings including a splash mob for a corporate event canceled and we did not get any other bookings. Although I was able to focus on other areas of my business life for income, we adapted by doing flash mobs "in place" where our participants did videos of themselves dancing at home to a specific song and choreography and we edited them together in one video. This kept our participants engaged and also helped them get physical activity while quarantined at home. We are now on our second "in place" production called Flash Mob in Place for Essential Workers. Our aim with this flash mob is to thank those on the front lines risking their lives to save ours.

I am now at another crossroads, not knowing when we are going to get back to doing flash mobs for a living. Another step in the adventure of life seeing how things will unfold and adapting to change.

ABOUT AUTHOR

I am originally from Los Angeles California and I've been living in Las Vegas since January 1994. I own Flash Mob Las Vegas and I'm also a independent consultant with Tastefully Simple. I am the author of the upcoming book, "Wham Bam Facebook Events." My passions are dance, dogs, art in the outdoors.

ABOUT MY BUSINESS

Flash Mob Las Vegas is the premier producer of flash mobs in Las Vegas for corporate, private and community events.

Websites
www.flashmoblasvegas.com
www.whambambook.com
www. tastefullysimple.com/web/dlahav

Facebook Personal Pages
Flash Mob Las Vegas
Simple & Delicious by Denise

Twitter
Flashmobvegas

Instagram
flashmobdenise

JUST WHEN YOU THINK YOU'VE

GOT IT ALL FIGURED OUT

The choice and perspective.

"Becoming the real you- you know... the one you want to be, even when you don't know what that is."
- Jennifer Fonfara

JENNIFER FONFARA

Let's get real, the actual truth of the matter is, no one's really got it figured out just yet. (A helpless Alanis Morrisette Reference, of which you'll find a few I am sure.) You see those women walking down the street, hanging in coffee shops, running down the sidewalk with their husbands wearing some brand-named whatnot and their beats headphones and their fancy ponytails... Or, how about the ones at CHURCH with the perfect smiles and dress to go with them? Or how about the ones at the School? You know who I am talking about, those MOMS who have their child's lunches perfectly packaged. God only knows she has written a love note to her kid with organic gummy ink pens so they can eat it after reading how amazing they are. Even those people have stories, and messes, of their own. BTW, when did this get to be a competition anyway? Why can't your mess be yours and theirs be theirs? Why do we sit and make up stories in our heads about how awesome every second is for them? Oh, you don't? Well then maybe this chapter isn't for you... I operate under the assumption that most people have an inner monologue that runs 24/7 just like I do. If you don't, well then cool. You do you. I'll do me, monologue and all.

READY – SET – ACTION!

When I am busy and productive my inner monologue is a good friend. It tells me things like, "That is amazing! You did everything possible and kicked today's ass!" and "Excellent job handling that tough situation, that was hard, and you were honest and as kind as you could by telling the hard truth to that person." When I let my guard down and get unproductive and idle, my inner voice can be the cruelest voice in the crowdby far, "You'll never be enough"… "You'll fail at this like everyone says you will" … "You are too damaged for anyone to want to work for" … "People in this town don't like you, why would they patronize any business you built?" Why do we do this to ourselves? Well, I am sure there are some fancy psychologists out there that can tell you.

One thing I know for sure is that when we do this it isn't helping anyone. Living into our best selves does not include negative self-talk.

Step 1- To eliminate this damaging behavior I had to admit to doing it. On occasion, I actually post it on social media to help myself knock it off. If realizing I struggle with negative self-talk can help one of the many people who follow me realize they are doing it as well, the "social media shame" or public nature is totally worth it.

Step 2- For me was all about setting boundaries for MYSELF. I have to be very careful when I get in situations where negative talkers are around. This means limited time with many old friends and family members and that has been hard to explain to outsiders. I've had serious discussions with myself about how much weight I give the opinions of outsiders because in reality, I don't OWE anyone an explanation. This is the opposite of how I was raised. I spent over forty years explaining myself and it clearly isn't needed. What is required of me is exactly what I require. Living up to my core values is my #1 responsibility. But wait, what are they?

Step 3- I've had to actually CHOOSE my core values. In Dare to Lead, Brene Brown urges us to choose 2 values from her list at brenebrown.com and wow, was this a mind-bending process for me. Frankly I could have just chosen Joy as one of my core values to start with because I know that is in my personal mission statement and I identify with that word wholeheartedly. But to narrow down the second I had to decide which other ONE would be able to help me SERVE the other things that were important to me in a way I could honor it. The second I narrowed down to was Authenticity. To focus on Authenticity would mean to eliminate even more things from my life and the top thing on the list was NEGATIVE SELF TALK.

Step 4- Identify where it came from to help it go away. For me, these thoughts started as a young kid. Most people blame others for thoughts that started young, but I'll take responsibility for putting these thoughts in my own head and letting them simmer. My mother had no idea I would implant the statement said in fun, "If you can't make the basket you can't play on my team!" and churn that until it came out as, "If you can't do it right don't even try." I truly believe that my mother and almost every mother does their very best to give, do, and be everything possible. She worked hard and loved fiercely, and I am proud that I inherited that from her. I also believe that all parents are HUMAN and no parent, regardless of all situations they coach through, do it all to the best of their ability. Therefore, taking responsibility to identify and eliminate is not a blame game or a shame game. It is my process to eliminate and be healthy. Some of the childhood thoughts came from situations I watched, some that happened to me and transparently, some I think I totally made up in my mind. I made up that my friends were lucky because their parents would all outlive mine. My mother was over 40 when I was born and my closest friend had young moms. (Mom turned 90 this year!) yes that means I am almost 50! Lol! I had to realize when something got me all riled up inside and it was a bigger deal than needed that it was time to look for a belief or thought I needed to eliminate. One of them that surfaced in the last few years happens when an older person, usually male, is upset with something I've done. I had to unearth why in the world I cared if my little old man landlord was upset my employee had turned the heat up and forgotten to turn it down. My Bonus dad got upset and would yell, and yelling= I disappointed someone= disappointing someone= someone doesn't love me= that someone will leave= I don't have the skill to survive without them. Silly, I know but being left was a fear from a childhood experience. Just ask my hubby what happened when I couldn't find the car in the Menards parking lot…

Step 5- Elimination of that fear. At times a fear creeps up in public, like the Menards incident. (seriously like he would have left me in the Menards parking lot an hour from home!?!) I do my best to use the tactic long ago taught by my mentor, Don Postle, to pull my emotion away and think clearly but at times I still fail and totally lose my shit. Yes folks, in case you missed it, I can totally lose my shit even in public. It's embarrassing but it happens on occasion. It plays into my core value of Authenticity but seriously... in public? I digress. After the discovery and some research, the honoring of the thought or idea and then eliminating of it. It includes really paying attention to what I say in the inner monologue and catching that thought EVERY TIME. I make a habit of making a physical mark on a piece of paper, or a drawing on my phone every time I catch it. Once I've identified how often I come across the thought I find a replacement and make a habit to say it multiple times when the old thought is discovered. Soon the thoughts start to change, sometimes I slip and fall backwards and have to get back up.

Negative thoughts don't help anything. Be nice to you. When it comes to the end you'll have to answer to the creator for all those mean words... After all, he created you because LOVE.

THE CHOICE and PERSPECTIVE

I believe input is important. Vetting what you input and allow in your mind, space and home will help you in great ways. Choosing HOW you see what has been put in front of you is as important as the actual content.

People- People- People

Becoming a successful leader is a journey I am still walking every day. I fail and succeed daily. Every choice makes an impact and when you think you're not making choices you are anyway. I've had plenty of mentors and encounters along the way that have shaped and molded me. I have stories and experiences that drive every step and help me decide what is best or right. My core values are my tracks and when I stay in them life is just plain easier. When I go rogue and forget to consider those values, well... life usually gets a little uneasy. I pray everyone in life has people who modeled WHO or HOW we want to be, whether they be parents or others they are the base of what we think and do. Here are some of mine in perfect "Jenny Miller" story fashion. One thing many of you may not know is that I've actually put in the work and won awards for actual story telling.

Be the person who is there, No matter what. This woman taught me almost everything I know (good and bad) and what I know for sure is that about 20% of those things I need to grab onto and 80% I need to readjust, mold into my life in another way or let go of all together. My first choice in my new life is to cherish the lessons I do get to keep, just the way they were delivered, I get to keep them. Mom always said, "If you meet someone and you don't like them, get to KNOW them." You'll soon find out WHY they are like they are and seeing them as a human helps you empathize, and empathy goes a long way. She taught me that flawless was a LIE we tell ourselves and the stealer of true JOY. Also that Judging others gets you one thing... Judged. -Thanks Mom. I Love you too.

Be the person who gives perspective to the things that don't really matter. "It's just Money. We will make more tomorrow." Believe me, after our second house fire this statement got me through some crazy thoughts. I didn't realize how engrained it was until My youngest son's senior year of hockey. He had speedily broken hockey stick after hockey stick. If you have been a hockey parent you know this is a thing... but seriously, THREE in as many weeks? We sat down for supper on a Wednesday evening and had the talk. "Please, be careful with this last stick. Things are really tight right now and I don't know that I can afford to replace this last one." Low and behold during that Thursday evening's game the last of the budgeted hockey sticks got broken. Skating to the bench I could see the disappointment on the big guy's face and the tears he was holding back. He sat on the bench and put his face in his hands, not wanting to look up and see my face. What had I done? taught my kid that money was more important than he? As the coach motioned to him to go back on the ice, he motioned that he didn't have a backup stick. (in this instance the guys would have just borrowed another player's stick and dealt with it later.) I climbed up on the boards and shouted in the best hockey mom style possible, "It's just money, We Will Make More Tomorrow! Borrow a Stick and GET OUT THERE!" His smile could melt the ice of any arena and that yell got one for the books. (and hey look, tomorrow came and more money was made, and another stick procured.) Thanks for the input brother John. 🖤

Be the person who believes in someone, even when they don't. You never know the impact it might have. Have you ever met one of those people that you just have a natural connection with? I was fortunate enough to have a bunch of coaches, teachers and advisers that helped me through adolescence. One of the mentors that made a great impact on my life was teacher, coach and cheerleader, Mike

Breed (personally, it still feels strange to call him anything other than Mr.). Do not get me wrong, I was no star athlete. I was not the most coach-able kid on the team nor I didn't have natural talent, but I do believe that most of the time I was a joyful and passionate player. (Scatterbrained teenager but joyful.) Coach was one of those people for me and I am very grateful for every moment of time I did get to spend with him. Anyone who knows me knows that I am no runner. But throughout my high school career I went out for the track team (Basketball which he coached as well for the beginning of high school and Volleyball as well) with little explanation as to why. I did not even understand the motivation but I knew that going out for a sport as bad as I was at it, was better than sitting home doing God knows what. There was something about the way he taught a class, something about the way he viewed us as students. No matter how poorly I had done he never tied my worth to the task. During one of my more or less memorable basketball performances I listened to the crowd cheering like it was the last few seconds of the quarter (There were really five minutes left) and I threw the ball at the hoop like it was really the end of the quarter. Needless to say, as a weak young kid, I missed by a mile and created a turnover. Embarrassed and very upset with my young self I went to the bench red-faced and in tears. At that moment Coach Breed said one of the most memorable things he ever said to me. "The next time you go out to the floor the only voice you listen to is mine. When you learn to focus you will achieve great things." Years later, at my high school graduation he shook my hand, raised his eyebrows and gave me that big chubby cheeks smile. As he did so he said these words. "Miller, we are expecting big things from you. Now go make me proud." This man, who had so much impact on my life, left us on my 32nd birthday. He will be forever missed. He taught us all many lessons but the one thing that almost every single one of us knew by the smile on his face was that the possibilities in life were endless. He was one of the very people that without being asked and probably without knowing it stepped up and took the place of a dad when I really needed one. Well Coach, you expected big things. You've left us now and I know for sure, someday I will see him again. On that day I will ask, "How did I do?"

Be the person who SEES someone and shines a light on the best of them- even when they feel 100% invisible. One of those for me was a quick and hearty friendship with an amazing soul, Betty Schoettle. This quick friendship was ended too quickly by a fight with cancer but in the few years I knew Betty she made quite the impact. Every second I felt like I was a gift to her. She made absolutely sure that you knew how special you were to her and that is a gift I can only pray to emulate. The most profound statement came at a high point in our relationship during a five-week sale in her country "barn" that Betty, her husband Ken put on annually. When she found out I had a background in merchandising we became fast friends. We could see the same patterns and art in merchandise. One day after she saw a display, I had put together she gleefully pointed out to everyone that came in that day that she, "had a new assistant!" At the end of the day she invited me into the house for a glass of wine and seeing as I was only a few miles away from the place I was staying I obliged. As we sat on the porch of their beautiful home talking, she asked many questions and we spent an hour or so getting to know each other better on a very personal level. Before I left that evening, she made one of the most random and profound statements of my life. "You stop worrying about who likes you and who doesn't." (We had never even breached this subject.) "You are kind and such a joy to be in the same space with. Keep bringing joy to those around you and you will soon be surrounded by people who love you." It was a comment that in the moment felt- nice but at the time I had no idea how much life she had spoken into me until much later. Betty was a light in my world, and she is greatly missed. Thank you. I pray that God help my light shine with the accepting grace and life Betty Schoettle showed everyone around her.

Be the person who stops the madness for another and speaks truth with love. Regina Brett said it best, "What other people think of you is none of your business. Be you and do it greatly." My philosophy is simple, "Drama is for people who don't understand how dirty their own laundry is. I don't want yours and you don't want mine so let's just lean on each other and be nice, shall we?" My oldest two children were blessed to be born in a family unit where they got to meet and have great memories with three of their great grandparents. One of which all of my kids, even those that weren't hers biologically learned to call Grandma Hazel. She taught me an important life lesson I pray to never forget when she said, "Life's is too short to be overly concerned with who belongs to who or who else is doing what. People who are nice to me get to stay here. People who aren't, don't. It's that easy." I love you too grandma. Blood isn't the only thing that establishes family.

Be the person who shows someone that it is ok to set boundaries for themselves. A few years ago, I joined a women's Connection group, Polka Dot Powerhouse. PDP has introduced me to many strong women. One of them, Dori Pulse, was talking at our chapter about boundaries and how they could help the sanity level of the boundary setter. The very thought of setting boundaries my life was terrifying and refreshing at the same time. I had always talked about the fact that I would allow this, or I wouldn't allow that but to actually follow through on what I would allow in my life was a goal I had never took enough action on to achieve. I had no idea where to start but for some reason that day it hit me that this may be the beginning of the major overhaul my life needed. Just imagine the shock of my husband the first time I said, " I won't allow that in my space. When that happens, this will be my response." The first time I followed through I think he thought I was going crazy. When you have lived so many years in a certain way it may be a good idea to give a little bit of grace to those that don't understand that these changes aren't going to be just a phase. Do not let them change your mind but know they may have a hard time adjusting to the new you. In fact, some may choose to leave the new you instead of adjusting to the change. Change is harder for some than it is for others. Life has always changed at an amazing pace in my life, so it is second nature for me to roll with most changes. For many this is not the case. Allow their boundaries as well. She also said "When you fail to put boundaries on yourself you open yourself up to the world's opinions. If you wouldn't say that to a stranger, you better not be saying it to yourself." Well Dori, four years later I am STILL working on this, Every Day.

Be the person who allows and sparks someone to continue to learn. Here I am, stuck- again... My friend Corey Janke tells it straight so when I'm a little stuck right now, I go right to his podcast and start searching. "When you're stuck it is generally because there's something you don't know" came right out of his mouth. Sitting alone in my office I spoke aloud, "Well, yeah... you are right Corey but what am I supposed to do about it?" (I was so stuck I couldn't even own it yet.) and then he quoted Brian Tracy- "all side skills are learn-able." So I am on a journey to discover whatever it is that I don't know that is causing my stuck-ness. (I know that isn't really a word, but this is my chapter, right? lol) Learning ends, in my opinion, when we die. I'm on a journey and I'm not perfect yet and guess what??? That is perfectly fine with me!

Be the person who speaks life in truth. Elaine Turso, another PDP friend but at the time total stranger, made an impact by challenging my very core thought. "Who in the Fuck taught you that you are TOO MUCH?" If you are blessed enough to ever meet Elaine you know she's transparent as F. She promptly read me- The Too Much Woman by Ev'Yan Whitney. By the time she was finished I was done for the day. I mean emotionally touched and overwhelmed as I had ever been. She literally spoke to every fiber of my being through this poem and that moment changed me for life. Please, if you've ever felt or been told you're just, "too much for someone/thing, go look this poem up. I've filled my life with the wrong people at times and for many I was TOO.... Fill in the blank. Whatever word you can come up with, more than likely someone has told me I was too much of "that." When the people surrounding you are lifting you up, and pushing you to greatness, you will be too.

Be the person that focuses another. Leader and Founder of our PDP group, Shannon Crotty is one of those for me. At times honing down and getting to the grit of things hasn't been my super-power but after hearing her philosophy on the "97% Suck rate," It took a few months to really implement a plan I was comfortable with but I'm holding onto this philosophy for life. She said, "You are blessed enough to be good at 3% of the things on this earth. Do Those." I am much better at it than ever. She's spoken many a wise word but this one… girl, I remember sitting straight up in that meeting and taking some serious notice! She was careful with her words and I felt immediately she was staring right at me when she said, "What the hell are you trying to do it all for? Don't you trust the people around you? Didn't YOU PICK THEM?" As I looked up I realized she was, in fact, looking straight at me- and the other 100 people in the room. She also brought these words to my ears for the first time, "When a person shows you who they are-Believe them." - Maya Angelou. SC, I love you girl. Thank you.

Be the person who supports another. Years ago, at a job I never knew would leave so much impact I met a fun lady. Loud, boisterous and jolly are words I would have used to describe her and in 25 years, those haven't changed. 5 years ago, when we started our escape room business, she was one of the first people who volunteered to help. She threw her hat in the ring and ever since she has been the reason that I make it through some of the hardest times and my cohort through some of the best. No matter how crazy the idea she can tap into my brain and use her hands to bring life to my thoughts, visions and words. She's driven what feels like a million miles, talked about this business and pushed me to be who I am today. She's supported me like I've never been supported before and there's no thank you or paycheck big enough. She's an artist in every definition of the word and is the most loyal human I could ever have been blessed with. If you have a friend that equals your crazy, supports you like this and never gets sick of you just the way you are, you better keep 'em. They are truly priceless. Anita Sykes, there are not enough words to thank you for your friendship.

Be the person who confirms another. Confirmation of the soul met in laughter, honesty and, at times, tears is a craft of my friend and confidant Martin C Haglund. He and his wife Sarah have modeled servanthood and the love of Christ in such an accepting way that I cannot attempt to explain. He's confirmed that it is God's will when passionate people lean into the 3% of things they've been designed to do. On one of our coffee meetings he confirmed for me that it is God's WILL that, "not thing one that can diminish your love for your children. No person, thing or act could or will ever make me feel any less in love with them and that is NOTHING compared to the love God feels for us." Oh, such good stuff.

Be the one who hones another and passes on what you've been given. Anyone that knows me at all has heard the name. He spent ten years honing my inner wild child, teaching me to control my emotion, forcing me to do what I thought impossible, teaching me that passion is a gift not to be squandered, that instinct is everything and trust in the Grand Organizing Designer is essential. Don (and Rose) Postle, the man who looked at me and said it plainly, "You gotta learn that your day is here, your emotions over there and the two must stay separate at times. We gotta put ourselves away and get this job done." and, "people don't have to like me or you for that matter. We have an eternal father to answer to and if He is happy, we've done our jobs… well."

If you are lucky to have met someone who could see your greatness through your mess, be grateful. ♥

"I hate the ladder and I don't want to climb up there."- "do it anyway."

"I can't deal with ____." "Do it anyway."

"I don't like to clean the parking lot." "Do it anyway."

Be that person who meets the excuses with no.

Be the person who deals and then Lets it Go. I believe that every action has a reaction. I also believe that once the reaction is over the most amazing thing you can do is let it end. My favorite book of the bible is Romans. "Beloved, never avenge yourselves, but leave it to the wrath of God, for" — this is the ground, the basis; this is the way you're able to do it — "it is written, 'Vengeance is mine, I will repay'" (Romans 12:19). I have 100% faith that He will prevail, and He will right my wrongs. An article I read on desiringgod.com said it very well, ""Okay, I won't count it anymore; I won't think about it anymore; I won't seethe with it anymore; I won't hold a grudge anymore." We feel like, "If I do that, nobody knows except me how bad that was." That's unbelief talking. God knows." Knowing this makes every decision easier to make, every necessary change easier to face and every day a new day. Walk away from what doesn't serve you and bring you and those around you joy. Create what you need and be great. I give you total permission!

In the spirit of my favorite book- Things I know for Sure by: Oprah Winfrey, here are a few- *"Things I know for sure"*.

One thing I know for sure is that everything ends. Every second, every minute, every hour, every day or year is an ending. Endings never stop. When the end comes, I want people to know I played, loved and lived to the best of my ability every minute of every day. If I could have one wish it would be to be remembered as a person who was sold out for whatever I was doing. Starting and ending with raising my children, no matter who I was with no matter where I was or what I was doing I gave it my all.

One thing I know for sure is that life is like a star shaped puzzle. There are going to be moments in life that the pieces don't fit. No matter what you do you can't trim the corners of the piece enough make it fit in the holes. (thanks Dad) These moments show up as disappointment, failures or hurts. But let's remember perspective. Just maybe we could look at this a different way? Sometimes things don't fit because they weren't supposed to Things come and go and we CHOOSE to hold on to some and let go of others. We can't hold onto a star because it's hot, too special, too big and too wonderful. What if we do what we can and TRUST that the rest will show up?

One thing I know for sure is that it is time to own my journey. At what point do you stop the blame game and start owning your life? When is it no longer what your parents taught you, what your siblings taught you, what your spouse taught you? When is it no longer what the world did to me? At what point do you stop blaming everyone else, giving them all credit, and start choosing what bounces off and what sticks and sinks into you instead? No one gets out of childhood without scars. (Side Note: BROKENNESS IS A LIFESTYLE & A BILLION DOLLAR INDUSTRY!)

One thing I know for sure is that I get to CHOOSE. One of the things I choose is the facts that I won't let "THAT childhood trauma" rule my life anymore. I believe the life is like a television and we are at the control. If you don't like what you are seeing, what's coming out of your mouth, what keeps showing up in your life, or whatever it is, then go a different direction and CHANGE THE CHANNEL. Do something different, say something different and make a different choice. The blame game is no benefit to anyone. Get over it, pull up your big girl panties (or your big boy boxers) and move on. If you don't like what you weigh, what you look like, the clothes you or the people you hang out with, change the channel. If you don't like the habits, you have picked up along the way- put your foot down with your damn adult self and **make a change**. If you don't like the way people treat you then stop accepting it. Sometimes life throws you a curve ball. Sometimes you have to, sit with a curve ball for a minute or as Rachel Hollis says for a season. And do the work to DEAL WITH whatever the curve ball was- or is and then please, move on. If you need help get it. Do Not stop until you've worked whatever it is out, and you can once again Choose to be you! Make the Choice, no matter what it takes. No, the world does not revolve around you but what you allow in your world does.

One thing I know for sure is that once a choice is made, Intentional Action will get you anything, anywhere. Go for it and put all of you into something and see what happens! Do Not Let Fear screw things up! Stop letting fear stop you and DO IT!

One thing I know for sure is that when you find joy in what you do it's easier to do it everyday. At times people call me a workaholic. I truly enjoy what I do. If I didn't, I would change it. Once you hit the sweet spot of enjoying the work it starts to become a lifestyle. Running our escape rooms is the culmination of everything my amazing husband Justin and I have ever done in our lives. Bringing joy to many and helping build teams has become a passion of mine. Justin's strong bonds to excellence in guest service and bringing people together make him the best partner for me. Now does this make it perfect and pretty every day? That bring us to:

One thing I know for sure is that finding the perfect person to spend your life with looks nothing like you thought it would. He is my opposite and yet carbon copy. My constant devil's advocate and my closest friend. Finding someone you can work and play with... now that is where angels fear to tread... Choose wisely and know that tomorrow the sun will come up and you will have to look at each other again. Those are my only words for it.

One thing I know for sure is that what other people think of me is none of my business. I have to do my best according to ME every day. What they see me do or recognize is hard for me to ignore. I am a bit of a praise junkie, after all, my love language is speech. I have to learn to praise myself well enough that I don't need others' approval OR their praise. After all, how is running a company, having an amazing bunch of kids and grandkid (soon to be grandkids) and being the best sister and guardian to my brother Bob good enough? I have to be careful to give myself enough care to keep all those plates in the air and, whether they like me or not. I have to answer to my creator and that is it.

WHO DO YOU WANT TO BE?

I believe that surrounding yourself with people who support you and making sure that starts with you, is the real secret to happiness. In our first anthology- Don't be invisible, be Fabulous, I told you the story of the socks and how it changed my life. That was a moment I surrounded myself with a team that neither supported me nor created the trust that could support anyone. Years later, I've actually built a model for filling your life, team and family with people who will make a great team and it applies in all areas. It is my ASPECTS model. There are many **ASPECTS** of a team and together these make up the strongest of them.

> Accountability
> Support
> Participation
> Encouraged and Engaged
> Communication–
> Trust and Tolerate
> Succeed

With these positions filled surrounding you, you'll have the support to get anything done. No matter what you do, where you are or who you are with- seek joy in the little things. No matter if the house if filled with toys, dirty laundry and loud kiddos, or perfectly clean and tidy. No matter if the job you do is stocking shelves, running a billion-dollar company or driving a bus. No matter what take time to find joy- every day. Be you and be great at it. Intentionally Love it- no matter what. You can do it!

-Transparently Me:
Jennifer Fonfara- Lover of life, the people in it and myself.

ACKNOWLEDGMENTS

As quickly as life changes, what we know friends and changes every day. Thank you to those who have supported me thus far and shown me that change is possible and always necessary. So many people took time to raise me up, all at different times in different ways. Without you all I wouldn't be me. Growing together with grace is the challenge and I'm ready to move forward. Join me?

ABOUT AUTHOR

Jennifer Fonfara (Fun-Far-Uh) Known as "Mother to three and Mom to many." Through the years, she has been mom to her children, her children's friend's, friend's children & most recently to her older down-syndrome stepbrother. She is the proud mother of two NAVY sailors & other 3 amazing young adults who amaze her every day. Jennifer is an American motivational speaker, human resources expert & has coined the phrase ASPECT Human Resources. Her motivation in life is to enhance the joy and experience of others. She comes from a background of customer service & management. She spent many years of her life devoted to Postle's Skate City in Rice Lake. In the 10 years she worked for them, Don & Rose Postle showed Jennifer how to lead by example, work hard, and use her passion in business to assignment her personality, drive & passion to its God-given potential. She believes that the challenges she has met in life were all put in her path to prepare her to be who she becomes every morning. On her path to success, she has earned MBA in business with a concentration in Human Resources & loves to help companies find balance while empowering their employees to perform to their fullest potential. She owns and operates Tactical Escape 101, a 5 location North Central US Escape Room Company. She invites you to follow her on LinkedIn, Twitter, Facebook and Instagram as her Denver Bronco fan status shows under her nickname, Broncosjenny.

ABOUT YOUR BUSINESS

Tactical Escape 101 is one of the original escape Room brands. Starting in 2015 with Jennifer and her husband Justin at the helm they've satisfied thousands of guests with great games and staff committed to safety and fun! Each location has it's own unique experiences! We are committed to being the best Escape Room Company we can be & value you- our guests and community. We offer a military discount to thank all current or past Serving military members.

Website
Tacticalescape101.com

Facebook Personal Page
https://www.facebook.com/broncosjenny

Twitter
@broncosjenny

Instagram
Te_101_ec

WILL HAVE THIS FOR YOU TODAY!

Making up my own adventures

"Alone = All One"
- an Old English phrase

ANNE CARR

How can you possibly condense 53 years of your journey into a few, brief words??!! I've spent the majority of my life choosing to take paths that very few others have the courage to. The paths less traveled. I take it personally that my Mission and purpose in life is to inspire and encourage anyone that crosses my path, to take that first step towards their dreams, no matter how scary it is. To believe in themselves. To follow their hearts. To begin.

On that note... Where do I begin? Where did I begin? I was born in the Australian Outback in a place called Broken Hill, also known as "The Silver City". My Mother's side is Croatian (formerly Yugoslavia), while my Father's side is English, Irish, and a touch of Scottish. It all worked together in a combination of loud, yet (mostly) self-controlled craziness. Big family gatherings, yet (mostly) prim and proper behavior. Lamb on a spit, yet you will eat the tripe.

I am not 100% sure where and when I became so independent, so determined to forge my own path and fiercely determined to blaze my own trail. I don't remember if there was ever really was one defining moment where I decided to stand on my own two feet, to be independent, to rely on myself, to take responsibility for my own actions, my own life. Rather there are small choices, adding up to large ones, knowing that I am ultimately responsible for where I am in life right now.

It compounded over the years. Small defining moments. I was, and still am, mindful of living a life I will not regret. To use every single moment that I have been blessed with to put to good use, to not waste those privileged seconds, minutes, days...the grains of sand falling ever so quickly through the hourglass. I never want to squander those precious moments on comparison with those around me, on gossiping, on lowering my energy vibe, on missing out on telling people how incredibly powerful and influential they are, encouraging and anyone that will listen that we all have our own stories to tell and voices to be heard and in turn, shared, to inspire others.

I have one Sister who is incredibly bright, talented and smart. She always protected and stood up for me when we were little. She still does today. My Father taught us both to be strong and independent, to fend for ourselves in a tough-love way, along with a mum who loved us, and still does, more than life itself in a true Croatian family fashion. My Mum is my rock. My pillar. The one who everyone trusts their most private stories to. The one who showed me how to be resilient and never give up on the ones you love. The one who loves me unconditionally. She is always there for me. I was fortunate to grow up with both sets of my Great-Grandparents. Full of love and laughter under the grapevines on one side and checkers and melting moments for Sunday brunch on the other. On my Dad's side my Grandfather passed away when I was young and I learned how to be independent and strong through adversity by watching my Grandmother. She taught me to always turn around and look at the back side of myself in the mirror before leaving the house to make sure I was presentable and everything was in place. I adored my Croatian grandparents. My Grandmother, my Baba, is still to this day one of the most generous people I know. She gives unconditionally and is always the first one to offer help to anyone that needs it. I always saw her working hard, and even to this day, I feel like she has more energy than I do! My Baba always reminded me to put on some "Lippy" before I left the house to make sure I looked presentable. My Grandfather, my Dida, was my ultimate role model in a Man. He left his birth country behind, along with his Mother, when he was 12 and never saw her again. He always came from a place of love, was impeccably dressed and I never once heard him raise his voice. He was the only man I knew that could stand in a room full of divided people and bring everyone together on a united front. He taught me, through actions, that every person is important and valuable and deserves respect, no matter their background. I think the one best word to describe him is kind.

I didn't realize until recently, after my Dad passed away, exactly how much I was brought up to be a strong woman. I was driven to Judo lessons to make sure I could protect myself. I was encouraged to participate in every sport possible. I was taught that if I didn't win a race to never forget to congratulate the winner. I was taught piano and even though I was not always a willing and enthusiastic student it is something I am grateful for now. Tie this in together with being a ballerina, soccer player, field hockey player, volleyballer, and anything that involved running around on a competitive team, sign me up. I was taught how to stand on my own two feet in a tough kind of love way, to be fiercely independent, to stand up for myself, and to respect and care for nature. To this day I still put spiders safely outside. I always loved being outside and I would help my Dad mix cement, hammer nails, clean out the bird aviaries, eat plums, and apricots straight from our tree. I would catch lizards with my sister and neighbors, keep them as pets for the day and release them again. Our family would often go camping, and I was shown how to catch and clean fresh fish and yabbies. When you grow up in a country with the most poisonous spiders and snakes there is not much that can phase you. All of this while living in a small but mighty, mining town which in and of itself had its own culture, foreign to anyone growing up on the outside. Isolated. Hot. Dusty. Dry. Full of dust storms and surrounded by saltbush, red dirt, and the Mundi Mundi plains. A place where you had 5-minute showers and always turned off the taps while brushing your teeth. A place I am so incredibly proud of, protective of and keep close to my heart. Broken Hill is currently the only living Historic City in Australia. Strong, independent, hard-working, fiercely unique, and full of fighters. Only someone that grows up there can truly understand the bush mentality. It made me who I am. It is a special place, the place I will always call home.

LEAVING HOME

I had to leave my home and my family when I was 17 if I wanted to go to University, so off I went. At the time it was a welcome escape to independence and freedom. Interpretation? I was not such a great student. Oh, I had a lot of potential and was very bright. I did not however take it seriously. Side fun fact, I had wanted to be a criminologist in the Police Force but I had to wait until I was 18 and it was suggested that I apply after my first year of college. I am still fascinated with that field, but I ended up taking a different path. That's a whole different story. In fact, a lot of my drive now is to compensate for my ignorance, naivety, and general lack of maturity that I exhibited as I graduated with more of a "degree in life" than I did in academics. On the flip side, and ever the optimist finding the silver lining in everything, I am still proud of the fact that I actually graduated with a degree, even though with much hindsight, I know I could have applied myself much more. I was young, bright, easily distracted, and definitely under-applied myself. My story though and my journey, and it all leads me to the person I am today. A person I am very proud of. I forgive myself for that phase of my life because we do the best we can with what we have at the time, and at that time I was young and immature with not much direction other than being stubborn and strong-willed and not listening to anyone that would offer advice. I never did like being told what to do…..funny….nothing much has changed in that arena now that I come to think about it!! One of my favorite affirmations now is "I Listen". I can proudly say that I am much better …and we are all a work in progress….. I am excited to continue seeing my progress!!!

I remember a close friend telling me when I was younger "Anne, you are not that important. Everyone has their own problems and worries and are focused mostly on themselves." At the time I was taken aback. I was a teenager and at that point thought everything revolved around me. After much reflection, I realized how much it actually freed me. In the big scheme of things, while I am important, I also am a very small participant in this adventure called life. In some small way that took away the pressure of thinking that if I made a mistake or did the wrong thing trying something new that it was OK. It wasn't going to be the end of the world. On the flip side, it made me aware that when I interact with people, when their focus was on or around me for a very small time then it was my responsibility to make the most of that brief moment and make sure that this time made an impact on empowering the person in front of me. Comments can be made in a fleeting moment and yet have a huge impact on the recipient, something I was unfortunately not very aware of in my youth and I cringe when I think of moments when I may have inadvertently made flippant, off the cuff comments unaware of how I left someone feeling. Something I am very mindful of today as well. Something I may not always be successful with, I truly believe most people are well-intentioned however we all do not have the tools to always say the correct things at the correct time. One of the strongest and most important traits we can adopt is the ability to realize that while we are important, we also must strengthen our energy to deflect the ability of the person in front of us to take away our power. To not allow any potential negative energy of those around us into our space.

I do remember the moment when I had finally had enough of being a guinea pig in my Psychology classes at University and constantly being used as an object to study. I hated that. It put my guard up. Then it became a game for me. We never knew when we were actually participating in a group setting so the older students could observe us and analyze our actions. I think this is where the final straw for me was. We studied norms and how people follow patterns and are predictable according to research. I decided that I never wanted to conform to a "Norm", to fit into a graph, to be an average statistic, to be classified as a number in the middle of the curve. I wanted to be the one that threw the curve off. To be on either end of that curve. To stand out. To be someone showing others that is OK to do and be new things. I stepped into myself through everything I did not want to be. I was not going to be judged for being average. I did not want to be boring. I did not want to be predictable in a lot of areas. I did not want to be categorized. I did not want to fit into the norm. I did not want to be tricked, studying an event for class and finding out after that I was being used as a subject to study for the benefit of someone else that I didn't know. I wasn't OK with somebody categorizing me that doesn't know me, studied me for 10 minutes, and had no idea who I actually was. Who the fuck were 'they" to analyze me based on such a brief limited analysis, decision, judgment, conclusion, observation they had made.

They hadn't earned the right to judge me. Their opinion wasn't important to me based on a brief analysis and it fuels my fire to do everything possible to not fit in, to buck the curve, to be the one that has to be thrown out because it skews the curve. I didn't want to fit into the "curve" so I vowed to make sure I stayed aware enough to stay out of it. I wasn't going to be put into that bucket. Nope. Not me. I wanted to buck the norm to guarantee I would never fall into a predictable state. I wanted to think outside of the norm, stay out of the norm, do things out of the norm, not fall into a life of routine that I would regret later. I want to be the one to make you question and think!

My saving grace at University was playing volleyball. I was All Australian for 4 years and earned a Sporting Blue, a very prestigious Commonwealth award. It kept me on a schedule. It kept me sane. It kept me physically fit. It kept me from self-destructing. To this day, I still say an affirmation from one of my coaches, "I am a one-er. I always do one more". I have carried that around with me in my heart since I was 16 years old and I use that for every time I want to give up. I used this affirmation countless times when I was training for my Black Belt. I also used it as a driving force when going after my 1st, 2nd and 3rd Black Belt degrees.

When you throw all those moments together in one big tumbler it is all of those. I watched. Instead of falling into the trap of creating negative habits and carrying them into my adult life, I looked at situations and decided that I would chase down the exact opposite. Oh, I definitely have my share of baggage still, but I constantly check myself. For example, I do not like arguing. It makes me cringe and I will always choose to walk away. I do not like conflict and will refuse to argue and yell. It is very rare to hear me react and while I am far from perfect, I do my best to diffuse situations. When my kids were younger, I was mostly reactive and took me a while to notice. I think having 3 kids can do that. You lose control and run mostly on reactive emotions. Getting back to the "maybes" of what makes me who I am or because it didn't matter, and regardless of outside opinion. Maybe it was because I am the second child. Maybe it was my father drinking when I was younger. Maybe it was growing up in a small country town in the Outback. Maybe it was having a father that made me, along with my sister, strong and independent and tough by showing us how to do things for ourselves. Maybe it was simply because I was born stubborn and fiercely determined.

MAKING UP MY OWN ADVENTURES

I am not sure if it was because I was encouraged to go travel, or because it didn't matter, and I was going to go anyway, but I do know I was encouraged to follow my Passions. The day after my 22nd birthday I left Australia to go travel around the world for a year by myself. It ended up being 3 1/2 years!!

In hindsight, I can't even imagine how my parents must have felt....but me...I was excited to be on one of the biggest adventures of my life!!!

All I had was my backpack, sleeping bag, pillow, $300, and a Round-The-World ticket...a ticket that allowed me to fly standby on 3 different airlines, in one year, as long as I was flying in one direction!! There were no cell phones...I didn't have a credit card...and I carried traveler's checks and cash in the soles of my shoes.

Before I left someone shared with me "The word "Alone" broken down actually means "All One" .... if you ever feel alone, turn that into "you are learning how to be All One, how to love being in your own company and learning how to rely on and trust yourself!!!" That carried me through a lot....along with random people I am truly grateful for. I met a lot of people, some who became lifelong friends, that helped me on my way and that is why I like giving back. I now like to offer my helping hand in return when possible. I enjoy paying it forward. While we can learn to love our own company we still need friends and family... and yes sometimes random strangers ..... on our journey as well.

If you are thinking you can't do something, or you're scared to try something new, or you don't fully believe in yourself, we're all one in those thoughts, we all have them, we all hold ourselves back....but imagine....what if you took that one small step....to becoming all one.....you WILL learn, you WILL grow, you WILL learn to trust yourself....you WILL be happy you did!!! A.M.A.Z.I.N.G awaits when you get out of your comfort zone and try new things!!! I am here cheering you on and happy to help in any way I can. I believe in you!!!!!

I remember calling Dad and asking him if I should come home and start being responsible. He asked me if I was ready to come home and I told him no. He said to me "You will know when you are ready" He was right. I did know when I was ready and as soon as I felt that, I returned. At that point, I didn't know then that I would end up coming back to the US to live. Fortunately for me, I had met the love of my life, my Soul mate at the two-year mark of my travels. After I went back to Australia, he flew over to see me. It didn't take me much to be convinced to come back to the US with him… 26 years of marriage and 3 Sons later, I am incredibly fortunate to be married to my best friend. He is my rock. He is my everything. Through thick and thin, ups and downs, highs and lows, happy and sad tears, growing challenges, learning lessons, running and building our business together, our 3 Sons that we are crazy proud of, still...and always...my Best Friend.

The world may keep changing around us but our priority for each other and our Family will always remain the same. We live by Family First and I am excited for our next 26 years... at least... of more Adventures to come!! We have our moments like everyone else, but our Family Mission Statement pulls us through everything. "Our Mission is to learn, live, love, laugh, think, give and grow, as long as it is good for the family because individually we are strong but together we are mighty" there's SO MUCH to be grateful for if you truly look around for the good.

Every morning as soon as I wake up... my affirmation is "Thank you Father. I am great. Thank you for this Beautiful Day. Thank you for my Family. Thank you for making me your Messenger. Whose life do you want me to make better today?" I never grew up with any "formal religion" but this feels right to me to say my Thanks every morning. Say your Thanks ....To... The Universe, Mother Nature, Earth, your Guardian Angel, your Soul, your God.....doesn't matter...say your Thanks. Be grateful. Help and give to others. I will never stop being grateful and saying my Thanks to anyone that wants to hear and receive it. Feel free to use mine if they resound with you until you can find your own.

I believe this is why I love being a Leader. I love stepping up and out and doing the things most people won't. To show others that you can do things no-one else will. That you get to decide how and where and when your life happens. You get to choose. Life is all about choices. Step off the "normal' train. Step off and look. Look to see where that path is going and if that is really where you want to go.

I love to show others to follow their own heart. To trust their instinct. To trust their judgment. To choose their own Dreams.

I read an article that on average, less than 10 people will cry at your funeral. That was a game-changer for me. Why do we spend so much time worrying about what others will think about us? The people that have more than 10 are the influencers. The ones that stepped up and out into their bravery against all criticism and judgment and followed their heart and soul to do what they felt they were called to do. To follow their passion.

Somewhere along our journey, we have lost something. A piece of ourselves. A huge piece of ourselves and that is our ability to listen to, and trust, our inner voice, our Soul, that is screaming out to us to listen.

STOP. TAKE A BREATH. BREATHE IN. BREATHE OUT. CENTER YOURSELF. LISTEN.

Occasionally she is a whisper. Every now and then she is an abrupt jolt. Often she is a tear rolling down our cheeks. Once or twice she is a scream. Mostly she is a deep sigh and clenched jaw. More often than not she is a little tug on our heartstring reminding us that she is still there. Waiting ever so quietly in the side wings waiting for the queue that it is finally her time to make her grand entrance, to step out on to the stage and into the lights.

What she wouldn't do for you to acknowledge her. She's tried. She has put people in your path, ideas in your head, flashes of greatness into your dreams, sparks of joy when you glance briefly her way, albeit fleetingly. Then.

She has moved back behind the curtains waiting for the next cue, again, to step out and into the music of your life.

We are all unique and our job is to find out what makes us unique. Start with stopping for 5 minutes. You owe yourself at least that. Do you hear that little whisper? Do you feel that little tummy turn? That inner cartwheel? A tingle down to your toes? That! There she is. She is nudging you. She is cheering you along. She is there for you and always will be. So am I. Breathe in. Breathe Out. It's time.

What are you telling yourself? What are you programming yourself to do, to be to say, every second of every day? You must be your own best advocate. In a world full of people taking the easy way, being critical, judgmental, you must be programming yourself. You must be the light. You must choose to shine bright and be full of love for yourself.

We are all given our physical characteristics at birth. Yet what we do with those is entirely up to us. We can choose to fight against it or we can choose to love ourselves for what we are. Beautiful souls, beautiful balls of energy.

Another of my current favorite affirmations came to me early one morning as I was lying in bed long before the sun rose. "With these hands and with this heart I can choose to change the world." It came to me in the stillness of the dawn and I was listening.

What if you don't even know where to start? Where do I start? Where do I begin when I don't know what I want to do with my life yet? Everything is figuroutable if you quieten yourself enough to listen.

My motto has always been "Try one new thing every

day" I know. I know. I fought the word "try" myself for years!! When I was younger, I lived by Yoda saying 'Do, or Do Not. There is no Try". Then I realized that I was not as open to new things because I had programmed the fear of failure inside me. I did not want to do new things if I was not good at them …if I did not do it perfectly. Now, I tell myself that there is a time and a place to "Do or Do Not" …and to "Try something new every day and it's OK to suck at it!!"

Take a different route, go for a walk, watch a movie you would not ordinarily watch, be brave enough to talk with someone you admire and ask questions, make eye contact with strangers and smile, lift your eyes up. You never know what one small word, one small event, one small introduction, one small action can trigger an idea, a thought that will eventually lead to something big. Something life-changing. Once you make the decision to try something new watch how quickly The Universe places a path in front of you and how fast momentum escalates.

So. Do something. Anything. Take a deep breath and commit. Sign up for something that scares you. I hear you. I hear the same excuses myself. I have the same chatter. It comes at me from all angles too. Over and over. Start with a walk outside, in nature. Recently I signed up for a triathlon and of course, the little chatter started. "You aren't fit enough yet. You're injured. You are carrying extra weight. You will be last and everyone will be waiting. It's on a Saturday when I want to relax. I don't know what I'm doing. Why do it when you don't want to".....and then. My other voice kicks in and says.....5,4,3,2,1....GO (thank you Mel Robbins). Sign up before you can change your mind, "You will be more fit after this. You can walk if you have to. Do it anyway. This will help lighten your step. So what. Saturday is a good day to work out. Cannonball in. You will learn fast. Because it's good for you to get out of your comfort zone. Always." So. I encourage you to sign up anyway. There you go. Do it. I know you will be a much better person for it, regardless of the outcome!

If you need extra help, carry around a little reminder. Something that brings you back to the present and into action mode. We cannot control those around us, but we can learn to keep ourselves aligned. In the past I struggled how to move out of that, releasing everyone else's journey and instead focusing on my own self to set the tone as a leader.

I have a morning routine that I love. I get up at 5 am and do my Goals, Affirmations, and Visualizations. 2 things help me move into focus on the mornings that I struggle with staying positive. For me, one is moving while I do them. I am a very physical person and it took me a while to realize that sitting quietly for simply does not always work for me....yet! The second is that I hold objects in my hand to get the "feeling" better. I have 4 things near my desk, or on my person, that have an emotional strength connection to me. This is what I typically hold.

A Key that I send my new team members when they sign up, to represent "Unlocking their potential". My key reminds me of a key from my home in Australia. (it is on my Vision Board to get home more, so it helps bridge the connection)

A Black Shell that has a little hole in on it (imperfectly

perfect and perfectly imperfect) that I found on the Beach in Florida before Convention last year and meditated on (near where I actually touched a piece of the moon at NASA...I didn't even know that was possible. The feeling blew my mind and I can feel that again when I touch the shell). I had made a promise to myself about walking the stage and kept the shell and now each time I hold it, it reminds me of my promise.

A White and Gold Star that my best friend in Australia sent me that came with the message "Dream Big, go confidently in the direction of your dreams and to let your heart be your guiding star".

A Tiffany Rhino necklace my husband gave me for our 25th wedding anniversary. The Rhino symbolizes strength, charging through the jungle and having thick skin so when people tell me I can't do something I can brush them aside and keep charging!! On my Vision Board, I have a goal of rewarding myself with 2 Tiffany gifts. Thie rhino ties it all in together.

I am such a totally stubborn and strong-willed person, that these help bring me back to the here and now and back to my focus. Find what works for you and go with that!

BIGGER MISSION

My goal is to redefine the definition of the word Beauty and to teach us how to highlight our own natural and unique inner beauty and to stop the comparison game.

I am incredibly grateful for my body no matter what shape I was born with, what shape I was in during my youth when I was a National athlete, no matter what shape I was in after pregnancy, no matter what shape I am in right now and no matter what shape I am going to be in when I am in my 90's! My body has allowed me to walk on this beautiful Earth for over 53 years, has allowed me to be passionate with my wonderful husband of 26 years, has birthed 3 wonderful Sons naturally, without drugs and at home by choice, has allowed my hands to cup the faces of those I love, to hug and kiss and laugh and cry and crawl and jump and sing and dance for joy, has allowed me to serve and give back to others. I have been able to visit new and exciting places and experience adventures. How can I not love that? How can I not love my body? How can I not encourage others to appreciate and love themselves also?

THIS is why I do what I do through my business!!! We truly have NO IDEA what our friends are going through.

All I see are beautiful women and men that to me, are shining bright so brightly. Most begin super shy or reserved. A little bit of inspiration can go a long way in giving people permission to take the first step and slowly build confidence.

I do see greatness in you. I have no idea what is going behind the scenes...we never do. My job is purely to teach and inspire and help YOU see the best in yourself. Like my team does to their teams as well, I love seeing my incredible leaders go on to be inspirational and incredible leaders too. We create the ripple effect together. Together we can change the world. The world needs good people to be examples and show the way to others.

I used to be hesitant to share my love of my business until I realized it wasn't about me. It NEVER is. I'm relieved that I have learned to break through the "fear of rejection" of hearing the word no and sharing my love anyway. Of anything that is important to me. No matter what I am sharing. That's the best I can do. Offer a way to a different and better lifestyle, more options, an opportunity to grow in ways you never thought possible. ...and through it all, you will end up with best friends and business partners and trips around the world with our families.....like I do. THAT to me is priceless. I could not ask for more in life.

If I can leave you with anything, I will share with you, reflections I have learned along the way on my journey. Looking back. If I could say anything to my 10-year-old self it would be...Anne.....you are going to have a truly wonderful life.....

♥ You are going to say the wrong thing. A lot. You are going to say the right thing more

♥ You are going to fall down. A lot. You are going to get up more

♥ You are going to fail. A lot. You are going to succeed more

♥ You are going to meet some not so good people. A lot. You are going to meet incredible ones more

♥ You are going to think you are not enough. A lot. You are going to to be more than enough more

♥ You will have friends you thought you could trust. A lot. You will find your true ones more

♥ You will always give the best way you know how and for some it will never be enough. A lot. For those that love you...it will always be enough more

♥ When you are younger you will let others' opinions in. A lot. As you become wiser you will listen to and trust your inner voice more

♥ You are going to question. A lot. You will search your heart and find answers more

♥ You will experience so much love with your Family, your Husband, and your Sons. There will be bumps. A lot. There will be smooth sailing and a whole lotta love more

♥ You are going to question whether you are a good wife, mother, daughter, sister, friend, employee, boss, inspiration, woman ... everything. A lot. You are... and you will be... better than good. You will live your life with your heart and good intentions...the best way you know how. And that, Anne, is a truly wonderful life.

PS....Oh....and enjoy the ride because eventually, you are going to be a badass, sassy, unlimited, and unstoppable woman who will go on great adventures, push yourself farther than you ever thought possible, and inspire thousands. You are perfectly imperfect and imperfectly perfect. You will have to watch your potty mouth on occasion though!!! Now GO... the world needs you!!!

To say that these years of travel majorly influenced my life is an understatement. To wake up every morning and be able to say to myself "What direction to I want to travel today?" and 'Where do I want to go today?" is full of freedom and choice. Something that to this day, I still say when I wake up every morning. What is that you say? You don't have the same choices? Oh yes, you do. Maybe not in those exact physical terms, but you do one hundred percent in your head, heart, and soul. The freedom to be able to think wonderful thoughts, visualize your future, and to be in charge of how much you give and receive emotionally. I didn't say it is easy. It is possible though. Some of the most important tools my husband and I have learned, shared with each other and our boys and then with others, including those on my team is how to set goals, affirmations, and visualization. It is one of my many passions and way of giving back.

Allow me to share one story that I carry with me every day that has always been the most impactful from my journey and one of the main reasons I am so passionate about giving back. I was flying from Egypt to India and the plane stopped in Dubai, where we had to disembark and then get back on. I was standing at the counter, my passport being processed, when I was told I had to pay a $300 fee. To my knowledge, nobody around me was paying this same fee and I was very uneasy about the reasoning behind it. I had $300 hidden, but it was all I had on me and I started to question why I was singled out to pay it. It was not looking good and it was obvious that it was starting to show on my face which was worse. There was a Korean man standing behind me and he stepped up in front of me, handed $300 cash to them, and told them "She is with me". I have never felt so relieved and grateful. This same gentleman stayed with me until we were back on the plane and when we arrived safely in India made sure I had a safe place to stay. I asked for his address so that after my travels were done, I would be able to send him the money and fulfill what I believed to be a debt to him. He refused. He shared with me that when he was younger, someone helped him in a similar way, and this made a huge impact on his life. The person that helped him told him that if he ever came across someone that needed help to pay it forward to honor the gift. He always remembered that. He told me that I, in turn, was to pay it forward. If I ever came across someone that needed help, then I would honor his gift to me by paying it forward. It would be disrespectful of me to send him the money he had gifted me and take away the honor that he believed he was paying forward. And so it goes. Every time I gift something, I do it in honor of paying it forward and full of gratitude for someone that over 30 years ago took one minute to help a stranger through a difficult situation. I always hope in some small way that I am able to have the same impact on a stranger with no agenda other than to show the world that there are still good people in our world.

ACKNOWLEDGMENTS

To my best friend, my husband Gavin, and my 3 Sons who are the definition of courage, strength, tenacity, compassion, forgiveness and love. Thank you for always cheering me on when I get out of my comfort zone and encouraging me when I need lifting me up. I am eternally grateful for my parents, my sister, my grandparents and my great grandparents who were always there for me in my youth and gave me a childhood full of love and support, especially in those times when I pushed the limits, and who are always there for me now. For my family, my friends and my tribe, you know who you are, thank you for always being there for me.

ABOUT AUTHOR

Anne was born in Broken Hill, Outback Australia and graduated from Flinders University with a BA degree with a Double Major in Psychology and Sociology. She was a National level Track and Field athlete, Soccer and Volleyball player and made All Australian Volleyball for 4 years, along with receiving a full Commonwealth Sporting Blue. After graduating, she travelled around the world by herself for 3 1/2 years and ended up in Palo Alto, California. She studied Pre-Med, began Chiropractic school, then deferred her study when she became pregnant (She loves being a Mum so never went back!!)

Happily married for 26 years to her wonderful husband, Gavin and with 3 incredible Sons they have owned Stanford Chiropractic Center together for over 30 years and Anne has been a Presenter with Younique Skin Care and Make Up Company for over 6 years. Anne was the 2018-2019 Beauty and Style Diamond Trainer for Polka Dot Powerhouse. Her goal is to redefine the definition of Beauty and to teach others how to highlight their natural, inner and unique beauty and to stop the comparison game. Anne is also a 3rd Degree Black Belt and her husband was a professional Football player. All 3 sons are Elite athletes in their chosen sports. Anne's ultimate Goal is to Uplift, Empower and Validate every person that crosses her path!!!

ABOUT MY BUSINESS

As owner of both a Chiropractic Center for over 30 years and an online International Beauty Company for over 6 years I am on a personal Mission to inspire everyone that crosses my path. I give you easy, simple tools and teach you how to feel empowered and confident in bringing out your own Natural and Inner Beauty with almost immediate results. Having a combination of radiant skin along with high quality make-up helps us feel put together so we are comfortable and excited about life's adventures whether that is working out in the gym, going to the park with our kids, working a corporate job or on a glamorous evening out. Fabulous skin and makeup can be natural, fun, powerful, sparkly, sexy and everything in between. At every age, when we give ourselves permission for self-care, when we look our best, when we feel beautiful, when we stop hiding, we simply enjoy life better.

Website
www.AnneRachael.com

Facebook Personal Page
https://www.facebook.com/anne.carr.5

Instagram
AnneRachaelCarr

Facebook Business Page
Anne Rachael

THANK YOU!

Feel free to connect with me anytime for a free one-on-one consultation or follow along with me through my social media outlets for daily tips, tricks, tutorials and inspiration.

YOU GOT

THIS!

Dare to dream big!

"*If your actions create a legacy that inspires others to dream more, learn more, do more and become more, then, you are an excellent leader.*"
- Dolly Parton, actress and singer

LINDA TALLON

I grew up in Akron, Ohio. I was a sickly child. In Kindergarten I missed 29 days of school. I always hated school because in class I was always playing catch up. I was always behind. I loved the social aspect of school, but it was not fun for me. It seemed all of my life I always felt "less than" other people.

In my neighborhood, only rich kids went to college. I was not a rich kid, so my path was set for me. That meant I was supposed to graduate from school, find a job, find a husband, settle down and raise some kids. My two older sisters followed that path, but for me, as a child of the hippie 60's, I got out of high school and moved to sunny California with my younger sister. I got a job as a bank teller and fell in love with the "oh so wrong" guy.

We ended up moving to Las Vegas where I thought I was going to live happily ever after. That relationship didn't last, but there were other things to be discovered in my new desert home.

The 60's were considered the era of self-awareness and finding one's purpose. I would read and read and read. I was the self-help Queen, always searching. I was always wondering if there was something wrong with me, when I finally realized the only thing wrong with me was I didn't HAVE a dream! I was "justa" bank teller and felt that was all I was qualified to do. I didn't have a purpose.

One day I heard of a "sex toy party." How fun did that

sound? It was bedroom accessories instead of rubber bowls. I decided to have a party of my own and invited all my broke friends. It turned out to be quite a successful party and I asked the consultant how much money she would be making from the evening. I was a bit in shock that she would be making in 3 hours what it took me 2 weeks to make as a bank teller! That intrigued me and I was very interested in finding out more about this fun business.

I liked to spend money. I loved to travel, but my bank teller salary was just not cutting it. My car was getting old. I wanted to get a new car so I thought this would be the answer in earning some "play money." Announcing to my boyfriend (now my husband of 39 years) I was going to be doing these parties on the side while I kept my bank job and his response was "Don't tell anyone you know me. I have a professional job." I chuckle about that now.

I knew there was a market for this product. Not everyone cooks, I know I didn't. But I thought everyone must be having sex! Additionally, these types of products could not be purchased at the mall and no one wants to go to those seedy adult stores. The lady who did my party seemed to be a normal person and she was having a fun! When it was time to order, it was done discreetly, so each guest would have some privacy. That was great. I decided to sign up.

I have never spoken in front of people before. I also never sold anything before. I was not any good at either. One week after I signed up my sponsor quit. I had been a teller trainer at my job. I know when you wanted to become a nurse, you went to nursing school. If you wanted to become a lawyer, you went to law school. There was NO school to teach me how to sell adult toys! I never realized that no matter what you sell it's all the same. If you are selling cars, make up, or pots and pans the basics are the same. I did not know there were books about sales, there were all kinds of resources.

The company moved to Las Vegas and I applied to work at their office. I figured I would learn the ins and outs and it would make me a better consultant. I struggled and learned my lessons the hard way. I have a Masters Degree in Mistakes! My mantra was, "If THOSE people can do it and be successful, I can do it. I just have to figure out how." Again, always feeling "less than".

FINDING MY CALLING

Remember, I was a bank teller, a very conservative job. I also assumed everyone would think it was FUN. I was amazed at how many people shut down when the subject of sex was brought up. Soon after attending my company's training I learned so much and I dedicated myself to getting better and better. I was also really having fun and I liked it.

I had worked for that company for 13 years. I never had the nerve to leave the "security" of an 8 to 5 job. But I was doing pretty good.

Then a big shoe dropped. That company went out of business. Two of the top people in that company decided to start their own. One of them called me and asked me to be on their Board of Directors. Again, all of my life feeling "less than", because I was "justa" $2,000.00 sales person (which was mediocre) and I was not a recruiter, my first response was "why are you calling me?" There were many top sellers they could have approached.

The answer was "You are an honest person, you are not a "yes" person, and you have ten years of experience." That made sense to me. Nervous as I was I accepted. I was promised "down the road" I would be making a percentage of the company profits. So I thought of it as "my" company.

I was adamant about training consultants. I know as a part time business, not everyone could attend National trainings. It was a part-time gig for so many military moms, who had no one to watch their kids. Or people who took care of parents or had other 8 to 5 jobs. My idea was let's bring the trainings to them. I started a program called Travel and Train. The company paid me to teach the trainings plus expenses. In each kit was a DVD of my live party to show consultants how it was done. To this day, I can watch someone else's party and there is at least one line that I thought up or taught. That makes me so happy!

I knew what it was like knowing nothing about sales and how long it took me to learn it. Most direct sales company had very little training at that time. You got a box in the mail and the attitude was "good luck, here you go and make the best of it." There are still some companies today with that theory.

Up until this time I still looked at it as a part time thing. I was always "chasing the money". I again felt "less than" ....when something happened.

At one party, a woman entered my ordering room and said, "I'll have what everyone else is having." I had this questioning look on my face. She told me she couldn't have an orgasm. First, I was in total shock she was sharing this with me. I consulted with her on a few items and felt like a doctor, you know, "take 2 of these and call me in the morning."

The next day she did call me, in tears, thanking me. My whole life changed in that moment. All I could think was WOW! That same week, a second woman came in. She shared her story, "I have to tell you something. I was at a party a month ago and I bought some products to take home with me. I was ready to leave my husband and kick him to the curb but I bought these items to try. We used them, we started communicating and having fun in the bedroom. I just wanted you to know YOU saved my marriage."

What those two ladies did for me was show me my purpose, which lead me to my passion for helping women. Sex is an uncomfortable subject for many women. Where do you go to ask questions? I WAS where I was meant to be. I really was a teacher. I was helping women in the most intimate part of their lives. Sex is not the most important thing in a relationship. But if you don't get along in the bedroom it makes all other problems bigger.

I realized I WAS doing something important. I kept growing and getting even better. I eventually quit my bank job to focus full time on my party business. I was on the Advisory Board for 20 years. I earned 2 cars and I have earned more trips than I can remember. I went from being afraid of speaking in front of a few ladies at a party to teaching a class of 500-1000 consultants at our company trainings. I went from making $9.50 per hour at the bank to making over six figures. I also noticed that when my focus went from making money to helping women, I started excelling at my job!

WHAT'S NEXT

After 20 years of being on the Advisory Board, the company was making some decisions that I just could not put my name behind. I never did get paid a percentage of the company. There were some other promises broken. They started having different rules for different people. I know that was a huge reason why the first company we were with went out of business.

I struggled with the decision to quit the Advisory Board. I was told to "suck it up" and "ride the train" until it stops. After all, I was getting paid each month to be on the board. My ethics, my own personal standards, I just could not sleep at night knowing things were not right. I knew there was someone trying to push me and another board member out because we did not have a college education. After much careful deliberation I resigned from the board.

I was amazed at so many people that quit talking to me because I was no longer in a prestige position. People who I thought were my friends. I kind of went into a depression. For 20 years I put my heart and soul into a company. But I came to the realization. I am an adult. I should not have listened to promises. I should have gotten a contract like "grown-ups" do when it concerns a business. I thought a friend would never do me wrong. I thought everyone lived by the standards that I had. Within 2 years, the company was sold to the company I am with today. Our new company made an agreement that we would keep our teams intact when the purchase went through. I was thrilled because I built a heck of a team. I had ladies in 38 states. My team did over 7 Million in sales.

I was reaping the rewards of my team each month in a residual income.

It was at that point I needed a change. I turned 63, I was having some health issues, a knee replacement. Nothing says feeling old like a walker and a cane. My friends are all retired and not working. I decided to quit doing parties, but spend my time training and motivating others. Maybe It makes me feel relevant. I just know I have valuable information to give. I hope I can make a difference in someone else's journey to find themselves.

I love to travel. So that was the plan. I was going to travel, do meetings and teach how to retire from a direct sales company. I don't care if they are on my team or not. I have always had the theory, "the more you give, the more you get back." It's rewarding for me and I just love it!

I was never much of a recruiter because I never really looked in the long term. After all, I got into this to make a car payment. My 8 to 5 job paid my bills. This was just "extra" money. But when my team started growing and my checks got bigger it got my attention. When I saw the ladies on my team being able to buy a bigger house, or a new car. I saw them blossom as women. I saw some leave bad relationships because now they had the power and the means to do it. I love supporting women on my team in getting what they wanted. I love watching them grow and accomplish their dreams.

After 39 years in this business I have watched women come and go. So many gave up so quickly. The biggest part of any business and becoming successful is the determination to know you can do it. You will hit roadblocks along the way. However, it is like driving, if you hit a roadblock. You don't turn around and go home. You find a way around it, over it or beside it. You need to believe in you! You believe in your microwave every morning!

Here are some of the lessons I have learned in direct sales.

ASK FOR HELP

I read a book called the Survivor's Club. Statistics show that in an emergency situation 80% of people would die waiting for someone to tell them what to do. People hate to ask for help. In a direct sales company there is a lot of heavy competition. I always felt the more the company grew as a whole the more they would give back to us. It made sense to me for everyone to help everyone, whether they were on your team or not. You can only really compete with yourself.

BE GENUINE

Be yourself. Know who you are, and don't pretend to be something you are not. Do not lose your values when you are in business. It's like Judge Judy says, "When you tell the truth, you don't have to have a good memory." The reason I am where I am today was a person asked me a question and I told them the truth. I have always told people, "If you ask me a question, be prepared to hear the answer." I am very direct. I have always hated when someone said something and you sat and wondered "I wonder if they meant to say this, or meant to say that."

BE NICE-BE LIKEABLE

If you are nice, if you are likable, you can get away with a lot! In the beginning of doing business I didn't know a lot of the "ins and outs". I was not very good at customer service. Those were lessons I learned the hard way. I use a lot of restaurant analogies. (Maybe because I like to eat) If you go out to eat dinner and your waitress is just horrible. The service is bad, she is all over the place. You don't feel like leaving a big tip because of it. BUT, if she is nice to you and she is fun, most likely you will "excuse" her poor service and leave that big tip anyway.

BE SPECIFIC IN YOUR LIFE

When it comes to goals you really need to be specific. You don't walk into a restaurant and say "give me some food." You have to know what YOU want. If you don't know what you want that is the frustrating part. It is like a hamster running in the wheel. You are spinning around not knowing what you want. That is what causes most of the stress. If you don't know what you want how are you going to make a plan to get it?

EMOTION=MOTION

80% of a business is your WHY, only 20% is HOW. Most of the time the HOW is pretty simple. Your WHY is the thing that is going to motivate you to get up off the couch and make those calls. People go to listen to motivational speakers and they are high as a kite on energy....that dwindles out in a few days. But if you have a "WHY" that should motivate you to keep moving toward your goals.

WHO IS YOUR BOARD OF DIRECTORS?

If you are self-employed you need a board of directors. Even if you are in a multi-level marketing or a direct sales company, you need your OWN board of directors. Big businesses have them. I am Pure Romance by Linda and I have mine. Who are they? They are MY personal cheer leaders. I think everyone should have at least 3 people they can run ideas by, or if they are struggling to reach out to them. If you have situations on your team and you just want some feedback, you need these people.

TITLES

In a multi-level marketing company like mine there are different levels. I want to stress a title is NOT a symbol of self-importance! It might mean they are more knowledgeable, might have more money or might be older and wiser. But NO ONE is better that YOU! YOU can make it happen. Usually the only one holding you back is the one you are looking at in the mirror. YOU can reach your goals, YOU can reach BIG goals. It really comes down to HOW BAD DO YOU WANT IT? And what are you willing to give up to get it? Time?

My best advice in business is:

- Be respected then liked. – it is not high school. Not everyone is going to like you.

- Know your core values and never apologize for them

- Know your strengths and weaknesses. Play on your strengths.

- Make a mission statement for your life.

- There are 3 sides to every story, yours, theirs, and the truth.

- Power is knowing who you are and being comfortable in your own skin.

- Who are the people around you? What are they DOING to you? And is that OK?

- What is important in your life and are you making that a priority?

- Don't spend too much time or money on things that don't count.

- Instead of getting through the day, get something FROM the day.

- Take charge of your own life. Take responsibility for where you are. You ARE where you are because you WANT to be there, otherwise you would do something about it. Whether you are broke (and some people are just comfortable being broke) or if you are in an abusive relationship, WHY are you staying?

- Spend more money on the inside of your head than the outside!

- Remember YOU ARE ENOUGH!

- DARE TO DREAM BIG!

Now I am going to tell you a little about my business.

WHAT EVERY WOMEN NEEDS TO KNOW!

How do I describe my job? I am a Sexual Wellness Coach and a Romance Enhancement Specialist. My company's mission is to Empower, Educate and Entertain through an in-home party plan. In my 39 years as a Romance Specialist I sometimes have felt like a sex therapist, a guidance counselor, and a marriage counselor all in one. At our parties the most important thing is FUN! We entertain while facing some serious issues. We have a private shopping room for ordering, and in that shopping room....there are many issues that are addressed. I am going to share some with you.

1. Orgasms. According to Time Magazine, women

should be having at least 200 orgasms a year. We all know sex and orgasms are two different things. When you have an orgasm, you release endorphins into your system. You are happier, healthier and you handle stress better. When you have an orgasm women produce greater amounts of estrogen, which makes hair shine and skin smooth! It also cleanses your pores and makes your skin glow. Orgasms help you sleep and they also help with menstrual cramps. Orgasms stretches and tones up just about every muscle in the body and you don't need special sneakers!

I am sure you have heard the saying "Use it or lose it." This can be very true when it comes to orgasms and sex. If a woman goes too long without using her sexual muscles or being sexually active (either with a partner or on her own) her vaginal walls can literally collapse. It can cause pain and an inability to become aroused or have an orgasm! If you are having painful sex, we carry many products to help.

There are many reasons why things like this are going on. We change, relationships change, sex changes. It is recommended you use a vaginal moisturizer 2-3 times a week, such as Pure Pleasure. It is also recommended to use Kegel exercising. We also have several products that help to strengthen the vaginal wall, such as Ben Wa Balls and Exercise-Her. If you keep your muscles in great shape, you will have stronger orgasms, and more of them. As you get older and lose elasticity in your skin tone. Many women can get a prolapsed uterus. If you sneeze and go "oops", you need these items!

Recently I was told by a woman in her 50's "senior sex sucks." I told her she just didn't have the right stuff!

2. Lubricant. The number one reason women use lubricants is comfort. If you are taking certain medications, such as an antihistamine, it will dry your vaginal area as well as your nose! If you are stressed, you will not lubricate properly. Lubricants decrease friction and increase sensitivity. When you have sex and there is too much friction it causes micro-tears in the vaginal wall. Those micro-tears will heal and leave scar tissue. When you get a lot of scar tissue you lose sensitivity. The most important thing you can do for yourself is get a great lubricant! We carry the best, which is called Just Like Me, or if you are over 50 years old you need our Pure Pleasure.

3. Are you just going the motions? Are you not in the mood anymore? Does desire come first? Or does it happen after you have "set things in motion." Does this have to do with the "M" word (Menopause)? Possibly. Or we just can't find the time between running children everywhere, work, traffic, being tired all the time...Who has the energy for that! YOU are not the only one! We carry "enhancement" products for this, for both men and women! The clitoris has over 8,000 nerve endings. Start with "O", it is flavored and it contains an

ingredient exclusive to Pure Romance, TriPlex Tingle. It has a cooling affect.

4. Toys. If I hear at a party "We don't NEED toys", then I know I have NOT done my job. It has nothing to do with need! It is like adding whipped cream to Strawberry Shortcake! The Strawberry shortcake is great on its own....but WOW when you add whipped cream to it. We teach you how to introduce a toy into your bedroom. We teach you how to use them together as a couple. Men are very visual they like to see things. When he is using a toy on you he can see your reaction, he can see your orgasm, which is very exciting for men. Some men get nervous about toys, if you are nervous about toys try our Premier, it doesn't even look like a bedroom toy! 85% of couples today have toys in their bedrooms.

Premier is a "tickler" and is especially made for oral sex, either him or you. And it can be charged with a USB. Yeah, no more batteries!

Toys are not just for kids anymore!

I was watching Steve Harvey's show recently. His guest was Al Rocher and his wife. The Rocher's had just released a book called "Been There Done That." It is a book on relationships and parenting. Steve asked Al what were the top 5 things of importance in relationships. His response was, "Sex is 1 through 4, and who cares about 5." It is definitely important.

I remember sitting in a waiting room at the doctor's office. Oprah was on and a guest named Dr. Laura

Berman. She suggested to teach your 15-16 year old daughter the concept of pleasure. She recommended buying a clitoral vibrator for them. You could hear everyone in the room gasp. I thought it was very funny the reaction in 21st Century when sex is splattered everywhere you go! You can google this interview called Teens and Vibrators, March 26, 2009. I thought it was comical, because I think parents are OK with violent movies, but if there is kissing, or nudity they get all upset. I know this is the safest sex you can have. 3 in 10 teenagers get pregnant. TALK, TALK, TALK. Have the conversation! There are two things that are inevitable. Kids don't ever want to think about their parents "doing it" and parents don't ever want to think their kids are "doing it." But believe me it's going to happen! Be educated!

Here is a little history of the vibrator. In the late 1700's women were going to doctors for ongoing symptoms of anxiety and irritability. Those were signs of what they called at the time female hysteria. The treatment prescribed was a "pelvic massage" to induce "hysterical paroxysm"--basically an orgasm, which would restore women to full health. Dr. J. Mortimer Granville invented the first electronic vibrator. One of the first was manufactured by Hamilton Beach, yes, the company that makes blenders! It was used for facial muscles, indigestion, circulation. To this day they are used in neonatal units for premature babies' lungs. There was a movie called Hysteria which is the story of the vibrator. In the 1950's when the "blue movies" started coming out vibrators moved from the doctor's offices to the dirty bookstores. And the nickname "dirty" made people feel exactly that way about them.

If you watched Sex in the City Charlotte had a toy called the Rabbit. One of the first high end toys. When it came out it retailed at $140.00. They had to do an intervention to get her out of her house. She was addicted to her toy.

I have had women at my parties that their partners were disabled and their partner wanted them to have a toy. There are many medications that stop men from getting erect, sometimes high blood pressure medicine or diabetic medicine can have an effect.

According to the American Medical Assoc. 25% of women have a hard time reaching orgasms. It can come from medical issues, to how you were brought up about sex and sexual issues. Recently there was news of a new "pill" coming out to help women achieve orgasms. It is something you have to take every day. We have creams such as "O" that help with this.

There are a lot of myths when it comes to vibrators. Here are a few:

1. If you have an orgasm by a toy you will have a hard time having an orgasm with a partner. That is totally false.

2. People think you need toys to "fix" things in the bedroom. I love when people say, "My sex life is fine, he satisfies me, we don't NEED a toy." Need is not the word when it comes to toys....it is just doing something different occasionally. I don't know about you, but "just fine" is NOT good enough! If

you go through the same motions over and over and over....it's boring!

3. Vibrators are for women only. NOT!

4. Vibrators are unnatural...It's not any different than using perfume, candles or lingerie.

We sell toys for women, toys for the guys and toys that are great for couples! There are toys you can both feel at the same time.

We teach you how to introduce a toy into your bedroom and use them together as a couple. Our parties are a safe environment to feel them, touch them, and purchase the items that YOU are comfortable trying. 85% of couples today have toys in their bedrooms. Do they use them every time they are intimate? NO!

Like everything else in life, don't be afraid to try new things.

Always make your partner wonder what the heck you are up to! Instead of your sex life being "just fine", head for HOT, HOT HOT!

Just keep in mind, if "those" people can do it, you can too! It basically comes down to how bad do you want it?

You can buy confidentially 24/7 from my website www.pureromancebyLinda.com. Are you interested in a fun job making full-time money in part-time hours? Or do you just have questions? Please contact me at gypsylsb@aol.com I would love to hear from you!

ACKNOWLEDGEMENTS

I would like to thank all the amazing women that have been with me during this crazy roller coaster of life!

ABOUT MY BUSINESS

Pure Romance by Linda is dedicated to Women's Sexual Health. We are an in-home party plan where women can relax with their friends and we show them the best in bath and beauty products, and bedroom accessories. Our goal is to Empower, Educate and Entertain!

Facebook Personal Page

http://facebook.com/linda.tallon.7

Website
www.pureromancebyLinda.com

ABOUT AUTHOR

I was on the Board of Directors for a multi-million dollar company for 20 years. I have worked with training women to be their best self for a long time.

THANK YOU!

Are you broke? I will let you know a secret. If you don't do something about it, a year from now you will be in the same position as you are today. Make a change. Try something! If you would like to try our business, please contact me and I will help you with little or no cost to you to become a consultant. It just might change your life as it did mine!

I AM NOT A
UNICORN

This story is
for anyone
who has ever
felt not good
enough.

"*I would be
happy, if
only...*"
- Anonymous

MELISSA SNOW

Most of us have at least one moment we measure our lives by. After that, everything falls into the category of "BEFORE" that thing happened or "AFTER" that thing happened. What we don't always realize is how much control we have over who we become in the "AFTER." We don't always realize how many choices we have. We don't always realize that whether this thing breaks us or makes us it totally up to us.

One of my "before and after moments" came on November 4, 2008. The day before Barack Obama became president. I had just gone through the booking process at the Denver County Jail. The last step was to take off my shoes and socks and shake them out, so the guard could make sure I had no contraband. The door to the holding cell opened and the guard ordered me in. I hadn't put my shoes and socks back on yet and my feet stuck to the floor with every step I took. There was one other girl in the cell, curled up on the bench with her coat over her head, asleep. I sat at the other end of the bench with my knees curled up to my chest. I felt a choking feeling in my throat as tears welled up in my eyes. I remembered that on the way here my dad told me that crying in jail "wouldn't do me any favors" so I sucked on my tongue, a trick I had learned from Oprah to stop myself from crying.

About an hour later, I was moved to a different cell, where I climbed up on the top bunk and stared out the window. I had a gorgeous view of the Capitol Building, with its flags waving triumphantly in the breeze. The irony was not lost on me. I reflected on why I was here. I wondered how long I would stay. I had never been so terrified in my life. I thought I would never be able to sleep. The next thing I knew, I was out of my body, floating above myself, watching myself sleep when the cell door clanked open and the guard shouted my name. It was time for me to go home.

As soon as I got home, I stripped off all my clothes at the door and put them in the wash. I turned the shower as hot as it would go and got in. I could not feel the scalding water as it burned my skin. As the water swirled down the drain, my "before" life went with it. Everything I thought I knew about myself, about love and about the future was gone, just like that. I dropped to my knees in the shower and sobbed. The kind of gut-wrenching sob that only comes from extreme pain and paralyzing fear. The kind that only comes when your whole entire world has come crashing down around you and you know that nothing will ever be the same again. The kind of sob that makes death sound like a relief.

TIC, TIC, BOOM

My dream of becoming an English teacher was nothing like what the reality turned out to be. I wanted to teach middle school and ended up teaching high school even though I was only five years older than some of my students. The day of my interview, I asked about the curriculum and the Principal looked at me like I had just used a word he didn't understand. When I was offered the job, I was handed a key and pointed to a temporary trailer behind the school that was had nothing in it aside from some desks and an empty bookshelf. The school was considered "low-income, high-risk," which I quickly learned meant that most of my students came to school without eating breakfast. They had babies at age 16. They smoked weed between classes. They had bruises their parents had given them the night before. They walked home alone, down one of the most dangerous streets in Colorado, every day. They joined gangs in search of safety and acceptance. They showed up to class without even a pencil. They didn't care about their grades; they were just trying to survive.

Although it was nothing like I expected, teaching filled my soul and gave my life meaning. It allowed me to get to know the kids on a level nobody ever had before. For some, I was the only person who could see their potential. I was the only one who believed in their ability to become whoever they wanted to be. Teaching allowed me to become everything they needed but never thought they would have. Not just a teacher but also a mother, a mentor, a friend. I loved those kids with every ounce of my being.

On the outside, it looked like I was living my dream. I had friends, a cute dog, and a rewarding job, but on the inside, my heart and soul were a mess. I had finally ended a very long relationship with a man who most of the time seemed like he couldn't stand me. I dated here and there and then I fell madly in love with a married man. For over a year he promised he would leave his wife and for over a year he stayed married to her. With every passing day, my brain's worst fears were confirmed - I was not special. I was not important. I was not enough.

I told myself that I was devoting every dollar I had, every ounce of energy in my body, every minute of my time to my students because I was a good person who cared deeply for them. And although that was true, my actions were not completely selfless. Every night when the man I loved went back to his wife, I was devastated. I felt worthless and rejected. But every morning when I arrived at school, I felt important, special, and needed once again.

I bought vitamins for the pregnant girls and I brought breakfast for the kids I knew never ate it. I took them to get dinner between school and their basketball games and I gave them rides home at night after the games. I took them to church and gave them rides to the mall. When they needed money, I let them do yard work at my house. When they had nothing to do over Spring Break, I let them hang out in my classroom. They called me when they were drunk and needed rides home and they texted me when they were scared and needed someone to talk to. Some of them told me I was the only reason they were still in school. Some of them told me I was the only reason they were still alive.

I never saw any of this as a problem. I only knew that when I was at school, I felt loved and when I wasn't, I hated myself.

One day, I was texting with a 17-year-old boy, making plans to pick him up for church, when he said, "I want to tell you something, but I don't want it to change things between us." Subconsciously, I knew what he was going to say. My heart, so desperate for anything that felt like love, screamed, "SAY IT!!" but my brain made my fingers text back: "You probably shouldn't say it." Crisis averted. But when I saw him a few days later at a basketball game, I felt like I couldn't help myself. I was dying to hear that someone, anyone thought *I* was worth loving. So, I convinced him to admit that he "had feelings" for me. Somehow my mouth managed to blurt out the "right" answer - "I am your teacher, it's not appropriate, etc." but on the inside, my mind was racing. I felt beautiful. I felt seen. I felt valued. I felt all the things I so desperately wanted to feel. Then, a few days later, when I had to run home after school to let my dog out, I invited him to come with me. I told myself nothing inappropriate would happen, but on some level, I knew that was a lie. One of many lies that I would tell myself and everyone else in the days to come. Three weeks later, I was in jail.

CHOICE IS A POWERFUL THING

Once I knew I was going to be arrested, I called my sister to tell her what was happening. She screamed, "WHAT THE FUCK IS WRONG WITH YOU?" over and over into the phone. Then I called my grandparents to tell them what I was "being accused of," before they were blindsided by my mugshot on the news.

Most of my friends never spoke to me again, either because they had been told not to or because they didn't want to. I was placed on leave but resigned from my job before I could be fired. I couldn't have any communication with my students. I went back to my house when the search warrant was executed, but besides that, I never went home again. People sent my parents condolence cards as if I had died, and I sometimes wished that I had. The shame, disappointment, and hurt on the faces of the people I loved most in this world was often more than I could bear.

I had no idea how I would survive. I had no idea how my life would ever be ok again. Three months after I was arrested, I wrote in my journal:

"What kind of life will you be able to have now?
What kind of job can you get?
Who is going to love you?
Who is going to trust you?
Who is going to want you?
How are you going to be able to live with yourself?
Where will you find happiness?
How will you be able to go on?"

I had no idea what the answer to any of those questions would be. I had no idea that it was up to me to decide.

In June 2009, I was sentenced to 8 years of "Sex Offender Intensive Supervision Probation," a minimum of 10 years as a registered sex offender and mandatory sex offender therapy. When I began therapy, I was told that I was not allowed to apologize to anyone. My therapist said that my words no longer meant anything and that if I really wanted to apologize, I needed to do it with my actions. I needed to show that I was ready to take responsibility and that I was dedicated to changing my life. I knew she was right, and I knew I had a choice to make: I could drag my feet through the whole process, feeling like the victim and continuing to tell anyone who would listen why what I did "wasn't *that* bad" or I could be brave and open myself up to the possibility that I needed to change.

I wish I could say I chose to be brave. For the first few years, I chose option A. I put a lot of time and energy into believing I was the real victim and feeling sorry for myself. I felt angry, betrayed, frustrated, and helpless. I blamed everyone else for what I was going through... "If only I had been offered the other job..." "If only he had kept his mouth shut..." "If only the judge hadn't been such an asshole..." I believed that my consequences were unfair and that the restrictions that were being imposed on me would prevent me from ever having the kind of life I wanted. I could only see what had been taken away from me, I could not see what I still had. I could only see where I had lost control and not where I still had all of it.

Eventually, as I realized how shitty option A felt, I started to lean more towards option B. I learned "radical acceptance" - making peace with the past and its inability to be changed, and looking more towards the future. I finally decided to really dive in and figure out who I had become and how it happened. I wanted to know how my brain convinced me to make the choices I had made so I could be sure I would never make them again. I expected to do the work and make amends, but I didn't expect the work to change my fate. I knew there was no worse label to have than "felony sex offender" and I resigned myself to the fact that my label would always limit and define me.

RADICAL ACCEPTANCE

There weren't very many places I was allowed to go on probation, but a few years into my sentence I earned permission to attend classes in the community. It was one of the only ways I could get out of my house and interact with other people. It was one of the only places I could go where my labels didn't follow. I was just like everyone else I loved it. I took improv and Spanish and public speaking and jewelry making. I learned about boundaries and mindfulness and dream boards and singing. Then one day I decided to sign up for a class called "The Inner Beauty Journey." As I walked into the classroom that Saturday morning, I was kicking myself, wondering why I would ever sign up for something like this. I had no idea it would change my life forever.

The teacher was a Life Coach named Cheryl who had the most amazing energy. She asked us all to answer the question, "I would be happy, if only..." As everyone else answered with things like, "I would be happy, if only I could lose 20 pounds" or "I would be happy if only my husband wasn't such a prick," I thought about what I was going to say. I couldn't possibly say, "I would be happy if only I hadn't committed a sex assault." I couldn't possibly tell the truth...and then, there it was, coming out of my mouth. The room went silent. The women all stared at me. I wondered if I could grab my stuff and make it to the door before this room full of moms violently turned on me. Then a small voice next to me said, "wow, that was really brave," and the other women all nodded. Then, Cheryl said to me:

"I need you to see that your problem is not that you committed a sex assault. Your problem is the story you keep telling yourself over and over about what that means about you and about the life you can have."

It was the first time in all of this that anyone had told me I still had a CHOICE. I could still become whoever I wanted to be. I could still create whatever life I wanted to have. Love still was and always would be available to me, but it all had to start INSIDE OF ME.

I decided to spend an entire year having no communication with men other than my dad so I could really find myself. When I was ready, the universe brought me the exact right people at the exact right times to learn from and grow with. I discovered that I didn't have to believe everything I thought and I learned that I could feel my feelings without letting them consume me. I was able to repair and improve my relationship with my family. I made new, more genuine friendships because I was finally showing up as my authentic self. I put everything I had into my job as a Legal Assistant, which turned into a career as a Paralegal, which eventually allowed me to start my own legal consulting business.

I was building a new identity and a new life for myself, which is not easy. So often, we can't see that we are the only thing standing in the way of everything we want and deserve. We all have these thoughts and beliefs that are so ingrained in us we don't even realize they are there. For me, it was all about self-acceptance and self-love. I learned that all the things I always thought were "wrong" with me were actually the things that made me special and unique. I finally saw that I was worthy and I was valuable simply because I was me. I found that I was beautiful, even if there was no man there to tell me that I was. I finally believed that I was enough, even if I was alone.

I learned to love myself so fiercely that when an amazing man came along who also wanted to love me, I was ready for it. I was no longer looking for someone to complete me because I was already complete. I was able to attract another healthy and whole person and for the first time in my life, I was able to receive the kind of love that I truly deserved. Eight years later, I am still in that relationship and it is still unlike any I ever experienced before it. We communicate with each other, we encourage each other, we respect each other and we accept each other. We are both free to show up to our relationship every day as our true selves and we love each other more for it. But none of this would have been possible without me first learning to love myself.

There is so much freedom, peace, and power in learning to love yourself. When I truly realized how much happier I was, I felt compelled to help other women do the same. I wanted to reach the women who were still struggling with feeling "not good enough" and who were still unsure of their own worth and value. I wanted to find the women who were still "looking for love in all the wrong places" and help them realize that it started inside of them. In 2016 I went through training and became a Certified Life Coach.

Now, I get to spend my days speaking to women all over the country about the power of self-love. I help them realize their own worth and value so they don't have to rely on a man to prove it to them. I guide them into finding their own power, knowing that they alone control their own thoughts, feelings, actions, and results.

Although everyone has an opinion, I share my story without shame because I know that we are all so much more than the worst choice we've ever made. I still feel guilty about what I did, but I no longer feel badly about who I was or who I am now. I have found a way to turn an awful situation that hurt so many people into something positive that helps women live happier and more fulfilling lives.

The biggest thing I want you to take from this story is that I am not a unicorn. The freedom, acceptance, and love that I feel every day is available to you too, no matter what you have done or who you have been. You too are stronger than you think and braver than you know. You too will *always* hold the power to change how your story ends.

ACKNOWLEDGMENTS

First and foremost, this is dedicated to my parents, my sister and everyone who stuck by me, even when everyone else walked away. To Laurie Knight, for helping me figure out how to be a happy and whole person and for teaching me most of what I know. To Cheryl Bartlett, for helping me forgive myself, for telling me that I could still be a teacher, and for believing that I still had something special to offer the world. And to Steve, for being able to see past my bad choices to the REAL me. For giving me space to be my weird self, for supporting my dreams and for showing me the kind of love I always wished for but never thought I'd find.

ABOUT AUTHOR

Melissa Snow is a proud Colorado native and a graduate of Columbine High School. She received a Bachelors degree in English from Colorado State University and taught High School English for four years. After seeing the power of life coaching firsthand in her own life, Melissa became passionate about helping other women who are just like she used to be. She became a Certified Life Coach in 2016 and shortly after published her first book, "Ten Secrets to Having the Love You Want." She is a professional speaker and is frequently featured on podcasts such as Embracing Intensity, Inspired Women, and Build a Life After Loss. She currently lives in Colorado Springs with her husband, two cats and one very spoiled black lab named Peyton (after Peyton Manning). She loves her nieces and nephews, Mexican food, hot yoga, dad jokes, reading and anything pink. She does not love seafood or being cold. Melissa's long-term goals include opening a "Cat Cafe" and petting ALL the dogs.

ABOUT MY BUSINESS

Like you, Certified Life Coach and relationship expert Melissa Snow found herself continually dating the same man over and over in a different body. These men were narcissists, bullies, fixer-uppers and emotionally unavailable. She wondered, "Why am I such a bad picker?" and "Am I just unlucky in love?" What she found through coaching was that the answers to those questions could be found inside herself and that the solution wasn't as complicated as she thought. Now, she helps smart and successful women just like you get out of their own way so they can finally have the life and love they want and deserve.

Website
www.melissamsnow.com

Facebook Personal Page
https://www.facebook.com/melissa.snow.71066

THANK YOU!

You can get my book, Ten Secrets to Having the Love You Want, FREE by going to my website and entering your e-mail. www.melissamsnow.com

You can also contact me via email at mmslifecoach@aol.com to book a FREE discovery session!

UNSEEN

I want to be heard

"Bad girl, bad girl"
– Mom

NANCY ROTHWELL

Hello!! Anyone there? Can you hear me? Do you see me? Want to know what I think? Does my opinion matter? DO I MATTER?? Is my voice too soft? Are you too busy to notice me?? DO I even have a voice here?? Is there a reason you're not paying attention to me? Are you ignoring me?

Growing up as the "baby" in my family, I felt like no one heard me, no one saw me. I felt excluded, ignored, overlooked. I felt neglected, invisible, alone!! I felt resentful and forgotten. I remember biting kids when they wouldn't listen because when I did, I got their attention.

Looking through our family's "old" photos I noticed I was often in a car seat. "Did anyone ever hold me?" I wondered.

CONFRONT YOUR SHAMING VOICE.

I wanted to be noticed, cared for, important, accepted, and valued.

It seemed like I had to work harder and harder to gain any kind of attention. I strove for perfection but never received the attention I needed. OFTEN, I got blamed for things I never did and accepted blame as though I was the guilty one.

In our family, we pretended we didn't have problems. We didn't talk about our problems. We didn't do sadness.

Crying wasn't allowed. I remember hearing "stop crying or I'll give you something to cry about." "That's enough crying now." I do remember, I definitely got noticed when I did something "bad." My first recollection of this happening was when I was about 3 years old.

I was out with my Mom at JC Penney one day. She was clothes shopping and I decided I would "hide" in the middle of the round clothes rack and see if she could find me. The only problem is that she was unaware of the "game" I was playing. Finally, when I came out of the rack, my Mom was nowhere to be found. I looked and looked. Where are you, Mom? NOTHING! I WAS LOST!! I wandered around terrified. I called for her but she didn't hear me... I thought maybe she forgot I was with her and she left me behind. Finally, the "lady" in the perfume department whisked me up off my feet and proceeded to distract me by spraying every possible perfume on me. It seemed like forever but Mom finally came to retrieve me. I remember getting very noticed after this incident. I remember my Mom saying to me "BAD GIRL!! BAD GIRL!"

There were life-changing traumatic events that occurred throughout my childhood we never talked about or dealt with. Some events, as I got older, I kept to myself out of shame and believing it was not ok to discuss:

Age 4 or 5: I was sitting in my father's truck while he was unloading dirt from the bed. I shifted the truck in reverse and almost ran him over.

Age 7- Watched my friend Mikey get hit by a car while he was on his way across the street to see me. I thought he was going to die and it was going to be my fault.

Age 7- I smoked my first cigarette and eventually became addicted to smoking.

Age 8- Had gasoline splashed in my eye by a friend. My parents put me in the bathtub and dosed me with water. I feared I would lose my sight, they seemed unconcerned.

Age 8- I nearly drowned at a pool where no lifeguards were present. My friend and I got out too deep and couldn't get to the side. She kept pushing me under as she tried staying above water. I was afraid I was not going to make it.

Age 8- My father hosted a party for his employees on New Year Eve at our house and I remember taking my first sip of alcohol. I loved the euphoric feeling it gave me.

Age 9- We returned home from a fishing trip and our dog ran out of our house and got hit by a car. His eye was hanging out of his head. We didn't think he would survive.

Age 9- Missed the majority of 4th grade as I stayed home "sick". Would make myself feel ill by laying on my stomach and claim I had a stomach ache. My Mom paid attention to me when I was sick. She doted on me. She made me lunch and checked on me. I got to watch the tv shows I wanted to watch.

Age 9: My Mom sent bean with bacon soup to Girl Scouts with me and I got bullied for it.

Age 12- Nancy Jo, my best friend since kindergarten, was diagnosed with Ewing Sarcoma Cancer, and went through chemotherapy. I was terrified she was not going to make it

Age 13- My principal started calling me "Moose" (I later learned the reason. He said when Moose see something they want, they go to any length to get it and that's how I was.) I thought he called me that because of my weight.

Age 14- I was babysitting at our neighbor's house and noticed all of their alcohol. I invited a couple of friends over and we proceeded to get drunk while I was supposed to be babysitting.

Age 14- I didn't make the cheerleading squad at the parochial school I attended after being on the squad for several years.

Age 14- Made the Public School JV basketball team and was on first string as an 8th grader. The night before our 1st game, I was kicked off the team because I was not attending public school.

Age 15- My sister, who had always been my best friend, chose a boyfriend over me. I was crushed.

Age 15- Tried out for and made the basketball team at the public high school I attended. Spent the basketball season on the bench despite working as hard as everyone else.

Age 15- Gang molested by several guys (I thought were friends) Inappropriate touching under clothing while in our fort in my parent's basement.

Age 15- A friend introduced me to huffing. I loved the feeling it gave me.

Age 15: My nephew had back surgery and lived with us for aa period of time. My Mom paid a lot of attention to him.

Age 16- I was on a field trip to the courthouse with my Government class, unaware that one of the cases was against my older brother. In front of 150 of my classmates, he was charged with possession of Cocaine.

Age 17- Crashed my car on a trip home drinking in Wisconsin. The friend I was with ditched me at the scene. I was left alone to face the police.

Age 17: On the night of my graduation, I drank a pint of vodka in an hour and proceeded to go to our all-night graduation party. There, I passed out in the bathroom and the police were called. I was hauled to detox where I woke up the next day.

Battled an eating disorder (bulimia) Junior High through my 1st year in college.

I grew up in a church where I felt like I was told I didn't deserve God's forgiveness. I felt shamed for everything I did wrong. Being told "that's enough" anytime I showed emotion (crying). I was never allowed to sulk or grieve. I was just told to move on.

I grew up with a father who drank beer daily. My brother, who was 16 years my senior, was an alcoholic. Our father had his own business and worked constantly. We saw him for dinner and when we prayed at night. Otherwise, he was always working. My mother was diagnosed manic depressive and was hospitalized on two different occasions for it. I watched her have horrible manic episodes.

THE DISEASE TAKES OVER

I started experimenting with alcohol during Jr. High. I remember stashing alcohol in my roller skating case and I'd sip on it throughout the night skating. One night after drinking too much I was fooling around with a friend and lost my balance. I fell against a brick wall putting a gash in my head. Throughout High School, when I had the opportunity to drink, I almost always drank to excess. I had to drink when I had the opportunity because I wasn't of age to purchase alcohol myself. My parents had liquor bottles in our garage so when I wanted to drink, I could usually find something there. As long as it had alcohol in it, I'd drink it. Once in a while, I could find someone who would buy it for me. Once I drank the first drink there was usually no stopping. Alcohol made me not care so much about what other people thought and when I drank I felt like I could be myself.

The week after graduation, I entered a 30-day inpatient treatment center for alcohol addiction. I had just turned 18 years old. It was 1984 and there were hardly any women in the AA program or hardly any young people like myself. My disease became who I was. Hi, my name is Nancy and I am an "ALCOHOLIC"... By the Grace of God, I stayed sober for 26 years. Then came June 2010. A friend offered me a drink one evening around the fire pit at our cabin and I thought "why not?" Maybe I'd overcome my addiction. I began socially drinking and seemed to be able to control how much I drank. I was quickly reminded how I felt once I drank. I could be myself and I really didn't care what others thought. Alcohol allowed me to "rest" to "relax" which I had a difficult time doing without it, or so I thought. I eventually turned to alcohol more and more in situations where I wanted to numb: when my feelings were hurt, I drank to find peace. I drank to escape. I drank to enjoy whatever activity I was doing at the time. Alcohol gave me what I needed to be okay with myself. When I drank, I didn't have to care about EVERYTHING all of the time. Drinking gave me the confidence to do things I would have never done sober. Over time I became obsessed with when my next drink would come. I couldn't imagine not drinking every day. At the end of the 6 years back drinking, I was hiding alcohol in the closet thinking no one knew. Alcohol became my solution to each struggle I faced.

It got to the point I could not do much without using alcohol first. I would drink before sporting events, weddings, graduations, evening church services, and evening exercise class. Drinking made ordinary household chores like cleaning the house and laundry easier to do.

The idea that somehow, someday I could control and enjoy my drinking is the great obsession of every abnormal drinker. I used alcohol as my "painkiller" for my Lyme's disease, a bulging disk, and after a fall. I suffered many times throughout my life in silence while everyone believed I was fine. I wanted whatever pain I was experiencing to disappear, to stop. I was hiding both the pain and the alcohol that I was using to cope.

There were days my will to die was greater than my will to live but what I knew was God had a purpose for my life. There were many times I wanted to end my life and would often think of ways I could make that happen. I was tired of life.

It was exhausting to keep up the facade, the mask and the hiding. I had gained a lot of weight and had stopped taking care of myself. Embarrassed to leave my house I withdrew as much as possible from everything. Retreating into myself and my addiction.

GUILT/SHAME

In January 2016, I watched my brother die of alcoholism. I would hear people talk about "fucking drunks" telling stories of others battling the disease, not knowing I was battling this myself.

After his death, my drinking increased and spiraled out of control. I was devastated losing my big brother. My husband and kids confronted me and plead with me to get help asking me to decide what was more important alcohol or them. I made the decision to start recovery again 6-12-2016. I had to come to the realization life had so much more to offer than this.

It was either get sober or keep going down the road I was on to my demise. If it costs you your peace- it's too expensive. I understand struggle. I'm saddened to think of how much of my life was wasted drunk and blacked out. Since getting sober I don't miss the regrets or blackouts or trying to piece together the events of what happened the night before. I don't miss the hiding, the shame, the guilt, the embarrassment of how I looked. Wondering what I had done or said while I had been drinking. I don't miss how sick I felt all the time and how unhealthy I felt both mentally and physically. I love being sober and being available to my family and friends all hours of the day.

Even though I felt alone, the truth is I was never alone. Jesus was walking with me through it all. HE was my rescuer. HE met me in my struggles and heard my cries. HE knew the pain I was in and now he rejoices in my recovery. HE didn't just fix me, he made me new again and is the cornerstone of my recovery. This little light of mine, I can now let it shine. I love the person I've become because I've fought really hard to become her. I am thankful to know that my story still isn't over yet.

I'VE LEARNED TO FIND CONTENTMENT

Everybody has opinions on drug and alcohol addiction, but until you've been in the pit, your opinion remains insignificant. Yes, people chose to abuse alcohol thinking they are able to control it. You don't control alcohol, it controls you. There are some lucky ones who have beat this disease but don't think because they're still alive that life is easy. Sobriety is an everyday fight to stay clean and sober. It's a constant battle from the time they open their eyes until they close them and it never goes away. Battling an alcohol addiction is a beast for the person addicted and the ones who love them. So, in loving memory of every family member and friend who has lost their battle with drugs and alcohol and to those who continue to conquer it, I offer this quote:

> *"Suffering is spiritual warfare. When you are suffering, it is vital to know that you aren't just fighting for the health of your body, or for a relationship, or against racism or injustice, or for your marriage, or for your reputation, or for your job. As you fight for those things, you must also battle for your heart. Suffering always puts your heart under attack. Suffering makes us all susceptible to temptations that wouldn't have had such power over us otherwise. Suffering is never just a matter of the body but is always also a matter of the heart. It's never just an assault on our situation, but also an attack on our soul. Suffering takes us to the borders of our faith. It leads us to think about things we've never thought about before and maybe even question things we thought were settled in our hearts. Too many of*

us, while battling the cause of our suffering, forget to battle for our hearts."
-Paul Tripp, "Suffering"

I've hesitated to share my story for fear of being placed in the judgment seat. I am done hiding! I've hidden long enough behind my shame. Shame doesn't live here anymore!! I want you to see me for who I am. I want to be remembered for my strength and recovery, not my addiction. I am thankful for the journey I have had because it is there that I have found the strength, courage, and qualities within myself I never even knew existed. I may have never sought sobriety on my own but have found beauty in it.

There was a time in my life when there was no way I could have ever understood the idea that there is beauty in pain, grief, or even depression. Once I decided to let go of what was no longer serving me and the parts of me that were no longer in alignment with who God created, it allowed me to be carried by the strength of my loving Heavenly Father. I realized I did not want to miss out on what God had planned for my life.

I am grateful for the strength and courage I found through the process of my pain. By no means has it been easy. However, there is a light, ever so dimly, waiting to be uncovered by each one of us in our own darkness. It is in this hope that we need to continue to search for the beauty within the pain, even in our darkest hours. We all have scars that delicately tell of the journey that has shaped us into who we are. Embrace your scars today!

Once I got sober, I realized there were lots of things other than just alcohol that I had to rid myself of anger, fear, resentment, and hate. Never did I ever think I'd be challenged with all that I have been, but I am grateful because the challenges have made me into the person I am today. Each morning I wake up, I remind myself that "I CAN DO THIS."

I am no longer hiding and invisible but instead I choose to be Fabulous!

ABOUT AUTHOR

Nancy Rothwell has been referred to as a serial entrepreneur. She launched her first company, Straighten-Up Organizing, in 2002 and has started 3 other businesses (Not Just Closets, A Bit of Everything, and Keto Journey Coaching). She currently holds the titles of Professional Organizer & Certified Keto Coach. Her husband Bryce and she will be celebrating 30 years of marriage this September. Together they have two children, Bryanna an RN, and Brayden, currently, a private pilot studying Commercial Aviation at the University of North Dakota. They share their home with their black lab Scout who is 3.

ABOUT MY BUSINESS

As a Certified Keto Coach with Keto Journey Coaching, Nancy educates, supports and encourages clients to achieve their weight loss and health goals using a Ketogenic lifestyle. She has helped clients get off anti-anxiety, depression and high blood pressure medication and coaches Type 2 diabetics who have been able to drastically reduced or completely eliminate diabetic medication.

As a Professional Organizer with Straighten-Up Organizing, Nancy walks alongside clients teaching them the process to get and stay organized.

Website
www.ketojourneycoaching.com
www.straighten-up.net

Facebook Personal Page
https://www.facebook.com/nancy.jensenrothwell

Facebook Business Page:

https://www.facebook.com/KetoJourneyCoaching/

Instagram

https://www.instagram.com/ketocoachnancy/

AN AFFIRMATIVE

PRAYER ANSWERED

I made a decision for my life.

"Don't be surprised at how quickly the universe will move once you have decided."
- Anonymous

LAUREN BROLLIER

I lived a really good life- I had a beautiful four-bedroom, three-bath home, a husband who worked hard and loved me, a great job as a Literacy Coach for a school district, and a small side business giving me spending money. From the outside in, my life looked perfect. If that were the case, why was I feeling so much longing?

When I was a young kid, I used to watch a minister on TV names Joyce Meyer. She wore eccentric, bold outfits, preached the gospel, and pointed through the screen at me, telling me to get my life straight. I loved her. I would think to myself; I want to do something like her when I grow up.

As a grownup, I still had the longing to speak on stages, to inspire people, to be a "businesswoman," whatever that meant. As a teacher, I figured the only way to do that was through education. Maybe I could become a superintendent, write a book, get hired to go to different districts, and speak. Or maybe, just maybe, this side business I had would take off, and I'd build a large team and a large following, write a book, speak on stages. I had dreams of something greater for my life.

I had other longings, as well. I had just gotten married a year before, and although I loved my husband and believed he loved me, I felt like we weren't behaving in a way that newlyweds would behave. I wasn't sure if I had been watching too many Hallmark movies, or maybe my expectations were too high, but I was craving more affection, more closeness. I could be paranoid, but it seemed as if my husband wasn't as interested in me as I would have liked. I kept a happy face on, truly grateful for what we did have. We talked each night when he got home from work, went to bed at the same time. He always kissed me goodbye in the morning. Maybe I was just wishing for something that only existed in a fairy tale.

A friend of mine knew about my deep inner dreams and recommended a book that would perhaps help me build my business. One weekend in October, feeling pretty good about life, but also feeling the longing for more, I started listening to this book, as I walked my German Shepherd through the fallen leaves and changing colors.

The book spoke to me from the first chapter. It talked about the subconscious mind and how it emotionalizes everything we feed it. In order to have better results, we needed to feed it something different. The author suggested creating affirmations about what we wanted to create, to make our mind believe we already have it and therefore, act accordingly. I could do that! Simple and easy. I wrote out ten affirmations as follows:

✓ *I am leading a team of women as they grow their businesses and improve their lives*
✓ *I live my life with passion and purpose and go to sleep excited for what the next day brings*
✓ *I am a Diamond in my company making $25k a month*
✓ *So many people want the products that I have prospects contacting me daily*
✓ *I give 10% of my salary to charities I care about*

- ✓ *My husband and I grow deeper in love every day*
- ✓ *We have a beautiful ranch home by the lake in Wyoming*
- ✓ *We grow together and make time for one another*
- ✓ *Our love is deep and strong*
- ✓ *We have an amazing sex life and I feel loved and cared for*

I started saying these affirmations on my drive to and from work every day. I thought back to a short period of time I had been to therapy when I was 19, suffering from anxiety. Stephanie, an older, kind, and straightforward therapist, taught me about using a replacement mantra. She said every time an anxious, dark, or worrisome thought comes to your mind, replace it with your mantra. At that time, my mantra was simple, "Not even gonna go there." She warned that I might have to use this mantra thousands of times a day in the beginning, but that it would get better over time. Boy, was she right. The first few days I had to say the mantra nearly every minute, but in just a few months, my crippling anxiety basically dissipated. I had my life back.

THE AWAKENING BEGINS

I took that skill and applied it to my affirmations. I was sort of an unconscious competent; I didn't know the science behind it or if that was how you're "supposed" to do it, I just did it. When a worry thought about my business would come to mind, I would say them. When a worry thought about my marriage would come to mind, I'd say them.

Within days, I felt a great internal shift. It was palpable that I felt more uplifted, more grateful, more confident, and more motivated. People who had never shown interest in my products in the five years I had been selling them, suddenly wanted more information. I felt more confident in front of my husband. I didn't care if he saw me without makeup or if he liked my decisions. A friend even gave me a free ticket she had to a seminar on the topic of affirmations and dream-building for January. This was really working!

It's interesting how we get trained to believe that outside circumstances have power over us, that they just happen "to" us and we have no control. This experiment was proving that I could in fact change outside occurrences through internal shifts and if felt so empowering.

A few weeks into saying these affirmations, my husband came home and suggested we go spend a weekend in Mendocino together. I was really excited. One, he was initiating to go somewhere romantic with me. Two, it was one of our favorite places where we went a lot when we first started dating. My affirmations were ringing in my ear. "My husband and I grow deeper in love. We make time for one another." This was going beautifully.

I didn't know it at the time I began saying my affirmations, but the number 40 is a symbol of transformation. In texts across religions, 40 days is what it takes to dramatically change, to show the passage of time, to uncover a new truth. In the biblical story of David and Goliath, Goliath challenges the Israelites twice a day, for forty days, to a duel. David, a puny little thing not even old enough to fight the war, catches wind of Goliath's offer, that if someone can defeat Goliath in a one on one battle, the winner would not only win the war for the entire Israelite army but would also be given the king's daughter as a bride and never have to pay taxes on the land again. David visioned a life like what would be promised him if he won, and the vision became bigger than Goliath. David defeated Goliath on the 40th day and won the war for the Israelites.

One night, 40 days into my affirmations, I sat in my home office, busily working on hitting a goal in my side business I had been approaching for quite some time. I had been stagnant at about $5000 in gross product sales for 2 years, and this month my goal was to hit $10,000 in sales. With this newfound confidence and motivation, I was getting closer and closer.

My husband kept coming in my office, asking what I was up to and then walking out again. He sort of paced at the door for a while. Finally, he walked in, and on this night he sat down on my Pilates machine, I thought of it as any other night. I was working on images for a Facebook event I was doing to promote my business and started showing him the images, proud of the work I was doing to finally hit my goal. He walked out of the room, and then nervously walked back in.

He said, "I think I might be depressed, I'm not happy." In that first moment, I wasn't sure what to say, although him being depressed wouldn't surprise me at all. That lack of passion, lack of zest, sleeping all the time, loner existence had never seemed quite right to me.

"I want someone to challenge me. Someone to make me go do things. I want someone to make me go backpacking or rock climbing." Wait a second, was this about being depressed, or about us? He said, "I'm not sure if I love you. You're not my dream girl." About thirty minutes before, I'd just eaten dinner, a big, greasy plate of Chinese food, mostly fried. My stomach did flip flops and I thought I was going to lose it. What was happening?

"So, what are you saying?" I could barely get the words out. I saw everything I had known of my life coming to a screeching halt, crashing into a brick wall. We had just gotten married, some of the gifts are still in boxes. We had a mortgage, and a house, and two cats, and two dogs. We'd just gone to a weekend away together two weeks before, where he told me he loved me and held my hand. What was happening to me?

I responded kind of stoically at first. "Well, if I am not the one for you, I'm not here to change your mind." But as he started to pack his things and leave for his brother's house, I started to cry and panic. "So, you come home and say this to me and that's it? I have to sit here and suffer with this by myself?" It felt so cruel.

I laid awake the whole night that night, and anytime I would drift off to sleep for a few minutes, I'd wake up in sheer panic, nauseated, and would run to the bathroom. At some point, I just laid on the bathroom floor. Was I the only person this had happened to? A husband leaving a year into the marriage? Why would he do this? My mind raced and yet thought nothing. My heartfelt like it wasn't beating. What was I going to do now?

The next day, I didn't go to work. I refused to text or call my husband to ask if he'd be back. When he'd left, he said he didn't know what he wanted to do. Maybe there was a chance of saving the relationship? All of a sudden, a thought popped into my mind, "I wake up with passion and purpose. My husband and I grow deeper in love every day." Ya, right. I thought. Then something crossed my mind. What if I was asking the Universe for a deep, loving relationship, and my husband isn't capable of that? What if this was actually a part of my affirmations coming true? It was an interesting thought. If he didn't love me and we couldn't grow deeper in love, then I would be okay. I filed that deciding thought in the back of my mind. If he came home and was done, I would be okay.

He came back later that day around 4 pm. I awkwardly waited for him to say something, to make a statement about where our lives were going. It was strange as if my life was in someone else's hands. Of course, I did not want to be with someone who didn't want to be with me, but I also meant it when I said my vows. This was not a casual decision. To me, if there was an opportunity to make the marriage work, I would do it.

We sat down at the dining room table and talked. Mainly, he talked about what he felt was missing, and how it was mainly my fault. I shared with him that over the last couple of months I had tried to fix many of the things he mentioned. He said he was sorry. So, for the next few days, we clumsily tried to pretend like nothing had happened. It made me crazy, but I tried desperately.

Thanksgiving morning, I made an attempt to save my marriage. I initiated sex. He rejected me. I felt about as big as an ant crawling on the wall. There was nothing left here. My husband and I put on a happy face and went to my parents' for dinner that night, mostly silent the whole drive there. It was the most harrowing experience of my life. Walking in the door knowing that my husband did not believe I was his dream girl and putting on a happy

LAUREN BROLLIER 133

face felt miserable. I played happily knowing that my husband didn't love me. I felt like a fraud. I wanted to scream out, "Do you know this guy married me even though he didn't love me? Do you know he's so selfish that he is trying to blame all this on me?" I was so thankful when my dad asked him for help installing a new front doorknob because it took away having to sit with him in the room and small talk.

The next day, I asked my husband if he had it in him to stay in the relationship and he said, "No. I don't want to waste your time." Then he proceeded to tell me all the traits a "dream girl" would have that I didn't have. I wasn't fit enough. I didn't go backpacking. I wasn't outdoorsy. I knew what I was, though. I was done. Done, done, done. That was the beginning of the end.

A few weeks later, I was at work, and messages started popping up on my group text with my best friends. "Lauren, do you know he has a Snap Chat?" My heart dropped because I didn't know that. This person who I was supposed to spend my life with and share everything with, had an app I wasn't aware of. It sounds like a small thing, but I had already felt like I was living with a stranger. We were sleeping in separate bedrooms at this point, and he was as foreign to me as a stranger on the street.

"Tell me what you think his password would be and I'll see if I can find out what he's up to" one of them demanded. I gave her all the passwords I knew he used. She easily got into Snap Chat and every secret he'd kept was laid out in front of me. My stomach dropped. I was an idiot. I had actually believed that he'd had this change of heart "naturally." That it had just somehow come to his mind but the change of heart had a name, and her name was Jennifer.

As I scrolled through his Snap Chat, I saw that he met her the weekend after we went to Mendocino together. They had had hundreds of "Snaps" including video Snaps. At my parents' house on Thanksgiving, he was talking to her via the app. He even took the carpet cleaner from our house and went up to her home and cleaned her carpet. Has your car or home ever been broken into? It feels so violating. Like some stranger was in your space uninvited. That's what this felt like.

EMBRACE YOUR QUEST

Knowing all that I was going through, a friend sent me this quote,
"Don't be surprised at how quickly the universe will move once you have decided." ~Anonymous

Wow. That's what had happened! I made a decision for my life. A decision for a thriving business, a loving relationship, and the universe had given me both. You see, on November 30th, the same month my husband left, I hit $10,000 in sales. I had no idea HOW my dreams would come true, but once I made a decision, the universe went to work on providing me with everything I had asked for. I was sure of it.

What I didn't realize when I began saying my affirmations on that October day was that my husband was the Goliath in my life. He was the invisible boundary between all things I visioned for my life and the life I was currently living. When I said my affirmations, it never occurred to me that the life I was visioning and the husband I was describing wasn't the one I was married to.

The universe rewards two things and it is proven time and time again by how successful people of all kinds became successful. The first is an abundance of thought. Your mind is like a thermostat that sets your outside results. When we set a thermostat at 60 degrees, the temperature in the room becomes that. Our inner thoughts are setting the thermostat for all of the results we will have in our lives. If our thermostat is set on a pattern of thoughts, our results will reflect that. If this wasn't the case, everyone would experience life in the exact same manner, everyone would achieve the same results. You already know that thoughts can create outcomes because nothing in existence was created without the thought of that thing. Unfortunately, humans don't leverage this knowledge actively to create more positive results in their life.

The second thing the universe rewards is action. If you take action, there is a greater likelihood that what your vision will occur, as opposed to sitting in a dark room waiting for something good to happen to you. Action is a decision. It's clear to the universe what you want when you take action on your vision. I had created an image of a life I would love living and that vision became abundant in my thoughts. I took action on that vision by deciding over and over and over again to decide I would live from the vision and not from the current conditions of my life.

Another thing that is believed across religions and over time is that we all have free choice and free will. We are not bound to any course of action. The universe, then, cannot make us do something. We all have the ability to do what we want when we want to do it. The universe waits for our abundance of thought and our action to put forces in motion to provide for us.

The universe rewarded me in many ways that Fall and specifically rewarded my abundance of thought and the action I took on it. When I faithfully said those affirmations, I could not have known that he would cheat on me and leave me, that I would move, that I would do all the things I've done since then. I didn't try to manufacture the HOW of what was going to happen. I simply had faith that something amazing was going to happen to me if I had the courage to believe it could. I told the universe what I wanted in my business and personal life. It delivered both to me.

So, how does one pick themselves up after something like that? Brene Brown calls something like this, "A face down in the arena moment." Everyone is looking, you're lying on the floor. How are you going to rise back up?

As the weeks went by and I found out more and more about my husband's double life, all sorts of lies he told, a feeling of violation would come over me, like I had been living with and sleeping with a complete stranger. But the more I pondered this word betrayal, the more I realized that the greatest betrayal of all, was that I had betrayed myself. I could think back to all the times something hadn't felt right, all the way back to six months into dating, when I had wanted to break up with him. "This is the type of guy you should like," I told myself. "Quiet, on the nerdy side, this is better than who you would normally pick." It was difficult to look back and realize that I had created this. I had stayed with someone I wasn't madly in love with. I had ignored the signs. I forced myself to stay with him when I knew something didn't feel right.

I would challenge any woman, or person for that, who believes that they've been betrayed, to look back and notice all of the times they didn't listen to themselves. There is no such thing as betrayal, except self-betrayal leading to unfortunate events. It's tempting to want to make my husband the villain in this story. If I made him the villain, I would have no dominion over my own power. If you think about it, the most loving thing that he ever did, was the act of letting me go.

So that January dream-building seminar I said yes to… It seemed right in line with my affirmations. I had no idea what would transpire just 48 hours later. Now that I was having to rebuild my life from the ground up, including a divorce, selling the house to my husband, losing my dogs to him and keeping the cats, moving back to my hometown, possibly changing jobs, I used this event as a lifeline, something to look forward to. I felt like it would help me gain clarity on what I wanted to do now that I had a blank slate.

All of December and January, I continued with my affirmations, just slightly revised. Because you know what? He couldn't take that from me. I was having to change everything, but I believe in myself even more now. I believed that my life wasn't falling apart but coming together. I, of course, had all of the anger, sadness, shame, and worry that comes with a dramatic life change and a betrayal, but I still knew that something better was coming for me.

At the end of January, I made it to the seminar. The speaker asked us to pretend we had transported to the year 2021 and everything has worked out exactly as we would love it, in health, in relationships, in career, and in time and money. As I reflected on what I wanted, I thought, I have a blank slate right now, why not vision for exactly what I would love to create? I couldn't lie to myself. Three years out, I would love a thriving speaking business that helps other women, a deep, loving relationship, travel, and thriving health. Just like my affirmations, I didn't know how it would happen, but I knew it would happen. I had created everything I had written down the first time, why not create it again.

Fast forward two years from that time. I currently have a thriving coaching and speaking business, generating over six figures each year. I have spoken on stages around the country, sharing this very story. I have coached dozens and dozens of women who are now living lives they absolutely love and I have met the most amazing, handsome, supportive, deeply loving man. Proof that the universe gives you anything you dream up and focus on.

✓ *I am leading a team of women as they grow their businesses and improve their lives*
✓ *I live my life with passion and purpose and go to sleep excited for what the next day brings*
✓ *I am a Diamond in my company making $25k a month*
✓ *So many people want the products that I have prospects contacting me daily*
✓ *I give 10% of my salary to charities I care about*
✓ *My husband and I grow deeper in love every day*
✓ *We have a beautiful ranch home by the lake in Wyoming*
✓ *We grow together and make time for one another*

- ✓ *Our love is deep and strong*
- ✓ *We have an amazing sex life and I feel loved and cared for*

I didn't stay in the same company, I didn't stay with the same husband, my house is next to the ocean, but I did absolutely create everything in these affirmations. Focus on the WHAT, let go of the HOW, let your dream lead you into better things than you could ever imagine. There is no such thing as betrayal. Only self-betrayal. I knew he wasn't the guy for me, I knew I wasn't happy, and I did it anyway because I was living small. Dare to live bigger, dare to see what is right in front of you, dare to lean into your longing, and you will absolutely manifest a life more beautiful than you could ever imagine.

ABOUT AUTHOR

Lauren is an inspirational speaker and transformational coach certified through the Brave Thinking Institute. She founded her company, Soul Savvy, to assist organizations and individuals, to build their dreams, accelerate their results, and create richer, more fulfilling lives. Lauren has spent over a decade as an educator and coach. She started her career in California public schools first as a teacher, then as a coach helping teachers to deliver the best possible instruction. Her ability to break down overarching success concepts into bite-sized pieces is what makes her a standout in her field. She has taken the stage with and studied under such names as best-selling relationship expert and author Mathew Boggs and international speaker Mary Morrissey. Through her coaching and speaking, Lauren has inspired thousands of people to live a life they love.

ABOUT MY BUSINESS

Soul Savvy helps people to deeply connect with their purpose, create a vision and discover easy, practical ways to live a life they love. To be Soul Savvy means to live at the intersection of your spiritual life and human results. We pride ourselves on giving people tools to live from the soul and be wildly successful. Our workshops, online programs and coaching programs are designed to help people create a quantum leap from where they are to where they would love to be.

Website
www.soulsavvy.com

Facebook Personal Page
Lauren Brollier

Instagram
@soul.savvy

THANK YOU!

I hope you found yourself inside this chapter, both who you once were and who you are becoming. Please visit www.soulsavvy.com/subscribe to download my free eBook Soul Affirmations, where I give you my favorite affirmations and how to use them to improve your life.

GO FOR

I T

*You just have
to choose you.*

*"I will go talk
to Bill"
- Eddie Viskocil*

MARY HANKE

I always knew I wanted to be a veterinarian. Since I was a little kid of about 6, that was the only thing I wanted to be. I remember going to my grandma and grandpa Kenny's and when the kittens were sick, I would treat by cleaning their eyes and noses. I would have my brothers, Tom and Bob help me, under protest. We walked to our grandparents, about 2 miles, daily in the summer. Every day, the first thing I did, was look for the kittens (the mom often moved them) and give them a treatment. I love animals and I wanted to help animals. My mom wanted me to be a nurse, she wanted me to go to Saint Mary's in Rochester, Minnesota, but I was going to Iowa State University and major in Pre-Vet. I can hear my mother's voice in my head, "Mary, you should be a nurse." She was fixated on me being a nurse, because that was her dream. She started nursing school, and was getting straight A's. She had to drop out because of no support or encouragement from my dad. He actually encouraged her to drop out, and she did, when I was about 10 years old. Despite mom's objection, I applied to Iowa State and was accepted. Once mom accepted my decision, she encouraged and supported me.

I clearly remember the moment I was accepted at Iowa State University, I knew I was going for Pre-Vet. My story is all about perseverance. My Dad owned a junkyard. For my summer job, I worked for my father in his junkyard, which was recycling re-rod and other metals such as copper and cast-iron. I was extremely upset when two weeks before I was supposed to go to college, my dad said to me, you don't need to go to college, you can just stay home. I'm like "and do you think I want a career working in the junkyard?" His words echoed through every cell of my body. The only thing I was able to think was, 'How dare he ruin my dream and stop me from going to college?' I burst into tears as my whole world was shattering. I ran over to my neighbors (who I have grown up with since I was three.) Ann Maria was one year older than me, (who I was planning on rooming with at college) and her sister Janey was one year younger, and we were together all the time. Their dad was the chief of police, Eddie Viskocil.

I was crying and said, "my dad says I can't go to college!" Ann was very logical, (and also wanted me for a college roommate), and said," I will talk to my dad". You all don't know this but my dad didn't listen to anyone. He was an Irishman and very set in his ways with his own ideas. There was probably a handful of people that he actually listened to or believed a word they said. One of them was Eddie, Chief of police of my little Iowa hometown. Eddie saw me crying, and his daughter Ann said, "Bill says Mary can't go to college". Eddie said, "I will go talk to Bill". We lived a house and a street away. So, Eddie went walking down the street and I stayed with Ann and Janey, waiting for his return. In one split moment, just like that, time stood still. Needless to say, I went to college 2 weeks later. (Many did not know the story of how Eddie made it possible for me to go to college, I told the story at his wake. He had influenced many lives, but that's another story.)

That was the defining moment of my life: life is a choice; it is what I choose. Ther was no way I was going to let go of my dream because it got hard or what someone else thought my life was to be.

At Iowa State, the change was big – huge, in fact. I found out Ann had an ulterior motive for me to go to Iowa State, she was going to terrorize me as my roommate. She's been at Iowa State for one year before me so she knew her way around. She was not going to let me sleep in, when I hit that snooze button she said, "Mary, you get up and go to class!"

NOT GIVING UP MY DREAM

At Iowa State, as a pre-vet student, we had assigned advisors out of the veterinary school. The advisor I had suggested that I think of a different occupation. My realization now is, he was saying to me," You are not worthy. You don't deserve this. You will never be good enough! You'll never succeed." In 1974, trying to get me to quit was based on me being a female. In those days, most veterinary students were male, and going to be large animal veterinarians. They would be in the agriculture industry. All I knew I was not giving up my dream because of what he thought. There was a knowing inside of me, a fire in me that knew that wasn't true. It's what I always wanted to do, and just because he was older, a professor in veterinary medicine and a man, it wouldn't dissuade me from my career in veterinary medicine. I am Thankful for the journey. We actually have input on how we create our own dreams, how we view things, and how we react. I really want to pass that on to other women, for any woman reading this right now that may be feeling helpless and hopeless in their life, please hold on. Hold on to your power. Hold on to your purpose, because I was discouraged several times by adults. One of them was my own mother because she wanted me to go to St. Mary's and be a nurse. One was my own father who wanted me to stay home and work at the junkyard. Sad to reflect now, knowing mom's dream unrealized. My dad just wanted me to stay home and not leave. I was not permitting my parents or anyone else to plan my career out for me. What this taught me "don't let anyone stop you from being you." If you have the dream that feels right to you, go for it!

I was what they call a two-year pre-vet, I packed every prerequisite into two years, and took a high credit load. It was a lot of studying and not easy coursework. When I got my first B it was hard on me. Yes, I admit it. I was quite the perfectionist. I was definitely used to getting A's all the time. Pre-vet was very competitive, and getting into veterinary school had 1000 Applicants and 120 spots. The % for two-year pre-vets, even lower. Most people don't get in. Before my class in vet school, the classes were predominantly men, going into farm veterinary medicine. My class was the first one (by law) that had to have 25% of women. There were exactly 31 women in my class of 120, (one extra of the 25%). Some men in my class started out resenting the women. After about one month, with the female teachers, and all of the classmates that were women, most of the prejudice subsided. We were judged by the strength of our abilities, and the content of our character, not our sex. One particular large animal veterinarian, a woman, comes to mind. You cannot restrain a 2,000 lb bull, no matter how strong you are. It is all about skill and knowledge. The men in my class soon realized how much they could learn from her, and some of the men teachers were incompetent. It had nothing to do with the sex of the person.

In those days you got a 15-minute interview and I was a nervous wreck. I'd gone up to the local shop on Main Street and bought a pantsuit. I thought I looked pretty damn good in it. It was definitely ugly now when I look back. I believe it was the most expensive thing I've ever bought up to that point in my life. I always thought the "Fashion Corner" was THE place and when you bought something there, you were going to be paying the big bucks. But this was a big occasion, my interview for veterinary school. To prepare for the interview, I was told they would ask me a few questions and that one of the interviewers was a crotchety old doctor on the board who typically asked the question, "what do you do that acknowledges every day that Jesus Christ was born?" Just FYI, it is the date. Everything starts a 0, and B.C. is before Christ and A.D. is after death. I was glad I had that little fact; however, he didn't ask me that question. I'd been working for my dad in the junkyard for the summer, so the question I got was "what's the most expensive scrap iron that you bring into the junkyard?" I was glad that I knew it was copper. I think he might even have asked me the price per pound, which I did know at that time.

The interview went well. I got my letter from Iowa State University, and I was a nervous wreck opening it. It said that I was on hold. I didn't get in, and I wasn't out. I spontaneously gave myself permission to let go. I had all my classes ready for the fall semester and was actually excited about the classes I picked. Some of them were fun classes like "scientific creationism" where they debate creation versus evolution. That sounded fascinating to me!

After a couple of weeks of not hearing anything at all, one week before classes were to start, I was in, I got the letter in the mail and it said I am in! I had been chosen. I was extremely excited, but I was only 20 and really was looking forward to the social aspects of college. I studied but the first semester I ended up getting a "D" in anatomy. I had to get eight credits of B or A to counteract that "D" or I was out. Another gal who did the same thing, Liz, we studied together all the time. We were told by our instructor that we should just drop out now. I can see how that moment, at that time, getting that 'D' was the worst moment in my life, yet was exactly what I needed to be able to be where I am now. Having my instructor say that I should drop out made me mad. That day I decided, I was not quitting. I also decided I was going to be a role model for women. No matter what I had to do, I would be a veterinarian. I had to bear down, my desire to get the 8 credits of B or A was stronger. It was very overwhelming, and I barely went anywhere. I put my fears aside and it was good to have a friend who felt exactly the way I did, if we were dropping out, they would have to drag us out. We studied our ass off and got eight credits of B and so we had a C average. I have followed my heart and intuition into the unknown with full confidence, I learned that goal + desire = success. One thing you might not know, what do you call the person who graduates at the bottom of the Veterinary class? We call them Doctor.

THE GOLDEN NUGGETS AND SILVER LINING

I wanted a job that spoke to my heart. As I look back to that girl who wanted to be a Vet – I'm proud of her and how she grew from the many challenges she has overcome. I didn't understand the freedom and gift I gave myself until much later. But then, most of us don't. You just have to choose You.

So many of us are told who to be, how to act, what to want, and who to love. We are bombarded by pressures, expectations, and little boxes we are supposed to fit into. Stop for a moment and shut all of that out.

Once you get there, ask yourself if I could be anyone, do anything, step away from this spot completely transformed into the person I have always wanted to be... who would that be? Ask yourself that question give yourself permission to honor and prioritize yourself first. You cannot give to anyone what you don't have yourself!

I hope to offer you faith to believe in yourself. Know that people will judge you, but it's what you tell yourself, that internal dialogue that really matters. If you have a dream, believe in it, believe in yourself. This will make your dreams become your reality. If you are like me, you have a "knowing" of what feels right to you. Follow your heart! Stay on that path of "knowing'. Remember, there will be challenges along the way, but no one can take away that "knowing' unless you let them. You can be whoever you choose to be. Be brave. Be kind. Do the work. You're worth it. Find and let your inside voice lead you. Trust your instincts and you will love who you truly are. You will find acceptance in yourself and therefore be accepted.

There will come a time when you look back and see

how it all unfolded. What might feel agonizing and hard right now, will subside to allow the golden nuggets and silver lining to appear. That is the richness, the reward, and your superwoman moment. It's where you don your cape because you overcame one of the hardest things in your life and you are a thousand times better for it.

All these years later, my life is exactly as I dreamed it. My work as a veterinarian doing a job I love; with animals and people I adore. I now share my story to empower women. I encourage every woman to value herself enough to be the author of her own story and to go after the life she wants with passion and perseverance.

ACKNOWLEDGMENTS

Maria Peth for introducing me to the Fabulous Dorris Burch!

My mom and dad for giving me the love that allowed me to follow my heart.

Ann Maria and Janey, two sisters that were my childhood friends, who told Eddie to talk to Bill.

Eddie Viskocil, for being such an upstanding person that even my dad would listen to him.

ABOUT AUTHOR

Born in Osage, Iowa. Graduate of Osage High School and on to Iowa State University Pre-Veterinary medicine, Graduate of the College of Veterinary Medicine, Iowa State University in 1980. Worked 10 years in the Minneapolis, St. Paul MN as a Small Animal Practitioner. Married and moved back to Iowa in 1990. Mother of 3 sons, 2 engineers, working and living on their own. Youngest will start nursing school in the fall of 2020. Married to Randy, also a graduate of Osage High School, a farmer raising corn and beans and elk.

ABOUT MY BUSINESS

Small Animal Veterinarian, self-employed, special interest in animal behavior, and helping with behavior problems. I also market a nutrigenomic for pets and people. It is for people like me, that want themselves and their loved ones (including their pets) to keep the vitality of youth. I love educating people about epigenetics, how with these products you can affect your genes in a positive way. I also am a certified Angel Reader, and certified in Transformational Therapy.

Facebook Personal Page
Mary Hanke
https://www.facebook.com/mary.hanke.16

Facebook Business Page
https://www.facebook.com/AnimalHealthCareClinicStacyvilleIA/

Twitter
Mary Hanke @BernadetteHank

Instagram
@Dr.maryhanke

Lifevantage
https://maryhanke.lifevantage.com/us-en/

THANK YOU OFFER

I offer free first time consults for pets, about anything, but have a special interest in animal behavior. I have a free course about Nutrigenomics/Epigenetics with a strategy session about maximizing you and your pets epigenetic potential. I am also offering a first time free session using my training in Angel Readings, and training in Transformational therapy.

ACKNOWLEDGMENTS

I am deeply grateful of every single woman who added her magic to this book.

This is the fifth book in our Don't Be Invisible Be Fabulous series – and I am deeply honored.

My whole-hearted appreciation starts with the readers and supporters of our first, best-selling book; they inspired the second and third and fourth volumes. This journey reinforced in my bones how essential it is to tell stories of real-life women triumphing in their lives. Thousands of women saw themselves in those stories, and then they could imagine a way forward in their own lives. So, of course, Volume 5, featuring more stories of hope and inspiration, had to be born!

Heaps of appreciation also go to the fabulous coauthors from our first, second, third and fourth books:

Thank you all!

WELCOME TO FAB FACTOR

Don't Be Invisible. Be Fabulous!

LEARN MORE

A whole new way of Being.

To reach your next level, let's tap back into who you really are.

If you've been around the Fab Factor Community for long, you know I'm deeply committed to guiding women to discover and LOVE their authentic power by allowing their fabulous femininity to lead the way.

Don't Be Invisible. Be Fabulous!

What does that mean? It means that you're so there for yourself that you increased your level of self awareness. This is not about self obsession. This is about self receiving because to the degree that you can't see yourself, except yourself, acknowledge yourself, honor yourself, celebrate yourself. Neither will the world be able to do so.

What a FABULOUS time to be a woman!!!

Everywhere you look, we're rising up, daring to do life differently, becoming the most fabulous versions of ourselves, and creating glamorous, innovative careers in the process!!!

We're craving deeper conversations with women who think BIG to prioritize our personal growth, our femininity, and what it will take for each of us to fulfill our uniquely fabulous purpose…

I am the fabulous Dorris Burch and my divine mission is to assist women in awakening to the truth. The purest, most fabulous aspects of who they are...

Here's to women empowering women and living our FABULOUS lives in the process.

Websites
TheFabFactor.com
FabFactorAcademy.com

Facebook Page
https://www.facebook.com/thefabfactoracademy

Instagram
@IAmTheFabulousDorrisBurch

Become A Fab Factor Brand Ambassador

If you believe that…

There is **Power** in the **Voice** in a Fabulous Woman…
There is **Purpose** in the **Life** of a Fabulous Woman…
There is **Passion** in the **Heart** of a Fabulous Woman…

Get your No Cost image at… BeFabulousImage.com

NEW FAB YOU SHOW PODCAST
LISTEN TODAY!

Don't miss an episode: NewFabYouShowPodcast.com
Subscribe and leave a review

Made in the USA
Coppell, TX
03 September 2020